Explosion at Orly

EXPLOSION AT ORLY

The Disaster That Transformed Atlanta

Ann Uhry Abrams

Published in the United States of America by
        Avion Press
        PMG
        175 West Wieuca Road
        Atlanta, GA 30342

ISBN 0-9724943-0-8

First Printing

Book and jacket design by Anne Richmond Boston and Richard Joulé.

Jacket photographs courtesy of The Atlanta History Center and The Robert W. Woodruff Arts Center.

Dedicated to the memory of

Adair, Ruby Mae Martin
Allen, Dorothy (Pat) Mills
Allen, Tom Chris
Ayer, Henrietta Collier Armstrong
Barnett, Paul Guerry
Barnett, Theodosia Lee
Barry, Anna Louise Earhart
Bartholomai, Emily Wade
Bealer, Elizabeth Gloner
Beattie, George A.
Beattie, Sarah Baker
Beers, Frances Haven
Benson, Sarah (Sally) Lowe Latimer
Berry, Anne Black
Berry, David Randolph
Bevington, Elizabeth (Betsy) Rickey
Bixler, Ella
Bixler, Roy
Black, Lydia Whitner
Blair, Elizabeth Montgomery
   Anderson
Bleckley, Katherine Caroline

Boon, Mary Mann
Boon, Dr. Harry M.
Brandon, Martha Pritchard
Brandon, Morris, Jr.
Brine, Dorothy
Brine, May
Brooks, Ruth (Dolly)
Bull, Ellen
Bull, Elizabeth (Betsy)
Bull, Elizabeth Barbara Wilmot
Bull, Frederick W., Jr.
Bull, Mary (Molly) Newcomb
Candler, Lucy Poe
Cantey, Elizabeth (Ted) Acree
Cantey, Morgan Sabb
Cartledge, Helen Lee
Cartledge, William A.
Cogland, William David
Cowan, Virginia
Crimm, Janet Fishman
Crimm, Reuben Gabriel
Cumming, Inez Parker

Cumming, Forest
Davis, Douglas H., Jr.
Dilts, Mildred Hodges
Dossans, Paul
Gerson, Mildred Wasserman
Gerson, Saul
Glenn, Grace Holding
Glenn, E. Baron
Henson, Beaty Wooten
Hill, Frances MacPherson
Hollins, Cecelia Cox
Hollins, Redfern (Red)
Howland, Mary Park Ansley
Humphreys, Mary Louise (Puddin)
  Bealer
Jones, Julia Lowery Block
Jones, Charles Baxter, Jr.
Kaye, Gladys Jones
Kaye, Arnold S.
Lanier, Nell Hunnicutt
Lanier, Thomas
Little, Charlotte Henderson
Little, Thomas Goree
Longino, Frances Stokes
Loomis, Louise
Luty, Marghretta B.
MacPherson, Clementina Marks
McDonald, Adelaide Porter
McDonald, Dr. Allen Pierce
McLoughlin, Jane Sharp
McLoughlin, Dr. Christopher Jones
McMillan, Ruth
Merritt, Anne Garrett
Miller, Augusta Streyer
Minier, Lillie Lee
Mitchell, Catherine Simms Potts
Morris, Ruth
Mulcahy, Anna
Murphy, Elizabeth (Betty) Carver
Murphy, David J.

Newcomb, Robert S.
Nutting, Margaret W.
Paige, Winifred Elizabeth Smith
Paige, Delbert (Del) R.
Patz, Florette Cohen
Patz, Louis
Payne, Annette Snelson
Pegram, Nancy Frederick
Pegram, Robert B., Jr.
Perkins, Mary Louise Martin
Prater, Homer S.
Pruitt, Emily Webster
Ragsdale, Raiford Moncrief
Richardson, Helen Camp
Rickey, Dell White
Robinson, Louise Phinizy Calhoun
Robinson, Roby, Jr.
Rooke, Birtie Hale
Rooke, William J.
Self, Joan Hallett
Seydel, Helen Clark
Shaw, Elsie Harris
Shaw, Charles
Sorrow, Edith Jackson
Stow, Ruby Robinson
Therrel, Bessie Pope
Tidmore, Alee Sutton
Turner, Louise Taylor
Turner, Margaret
Turner, Robert Pate
Virgin, Lee MacPherson
Wien, Ellen Michaelson
Wien, Sidney A.
Wien, Joan (Toni)
Williams, Rosalind Janes
Williamson, E. Lysle
Wilson, Virginia Dillon
Woolley, Vasser, Jr.
Young, Carroll MacDonald
Young, Sykes Harold

Contents

Horrific Déjà Vu

*L*ike all Americans, I was stunned and horrified by the appalling events of September 11, 2001. When the shock dissolved into numbness, I had an especially chilling epiphany. As the first plane slammed into the World Trade Center, I was writing about how Atlantans reacted when hearing about a plane crash that occurred at Orly Field near Paris in 1962. In a state of disbelief, I found myself spanning two unimaginable disasters: one national and global, inspiring intense patriotism; the other local and personal, causing a prolonged and gnawing sadness. Tragedy in whatever dimension is so incomprehensible that all rational beliefs are suspended. From experience, I know that from now on, the moment of hearing about the events of September 11 and my immediate reactions will be indelibly imprinted on my memory.

On June 3, 1962, my family was driving back from a weekend in Gatlinburg, Tennessee. My husband was at the wheel, my three young children screaming and fighting in the back seat. To quiet them, I turned on the radio. In those days remote areas like the Smoky mountains got very poor reception and the only station I could find blipped on and off. Suddenly the crackly, intermittent music was interrupted by a bulletin. We could hardly hear what the announcer was saying. But just before the station faded away again, I heard the words "art association" and "crash." I burst into tears. My husband was amazed, repeating, "What's wrong? What's happened?" My rambunctious children lapsed into shocked silence at seeing their usually composed mother so upset. It is a scene that the oldest of them—then seven—remembers to this day.

I knew in the split second of that patchy report that we had just lost some of our family's closest friends. I kept sobbing the names of our friends. Then I realized that their daughter, a girl who had been my brother's childhood sweetheart, was also on the plane. It was almost too much to grasp. We numbly retreated to Atlanta, learning as we drew closer that my worst fears had been confirmed.

An Air France chartered jet carrying 122 passengers (106 of whom lived in Atlanta) and a crew of 10 had crashed at approximately 12:30 P.M., Paris time. It was the largest number of people killed in a single plane crash up to that date. On board were returning passengers from a three-week trip to Europe sponsored by the Atlanta Art Association. Some had been on an escorted tour that began and ended in Paris with stops in London, Amsterdam, Lucerne, Venice, Florence, and Rome. Others had taken advantage of the inexpensive charter fare but chose to travel independently.

Witnesses at the airport saw the 140-ton jet taxi down the

runway and elevate about six feet into the air, then ricochet like a bullet back onto the runway. "It did not seem to leave the ground," said an airport mechanic. The fuselage convulsed in severe jolts. The nose plunged downward. Within seconds, it veered drunkenly across the runway, smashed through a low wooden fence, listed to the left, and plowed into a clump of trees. Sixty-three tons of jet fuel roared through the fuselage. Almost instantly, the charter plane blew apart and was transformed into a thundering inferno.

Back in Atlanta, there was a great deal of mutual commiseration, many tears. My husband waited in line at the neighborhood drugstore to buy a copy of the special edition of the *Atlanta Journal* issued hastily the Sunday evening of the crash. Only then, as I read the list of those aboard the plane, did I realize how hard our city had been hit. Not only did we know many of the people who died, but these were prominent Atlantans, businessmen and women, artists, lawyers, doctors, officials of the museum, and names seen frequently on the local society pages. In subsequent years, my life began to intersect with several of these families, their children attending school with my children, a friend marrying a widower whose wife had died at Orly, a niece marrying the grandson of a couple on the downed Air France plane. For the past four decades, the tragedy has hovered over Atlanta.

As I began interviewing relatives and friends of those lost, I felt more and more that the families appreciated my efforts. Unlike the tragedy unveiling before Americans in September 2001, there were no teams of chaplains, social workers, or psychologists trained as grief counselors offering their assistance to the survivors. There were no group therapy sessions. With the exception of almost thirty of the bereaved families who knew each other socially, most of the others suffered their losses alone. City authorities—especially Mayor Ivan Allen Jr.—were extremely helpful in offering official words of comfort, in pledging to return the bodies from France, in providing space to display and distribute artifacts found in the wreckage.

The rituals following disasters, whether affecting individuals or the world, are hauntingly similar. First come shocking news reports. We watch in horror the futile attempts at rescue and view the community grieving. This is followed by a remarkable display of courage by rescue workers and elected officials. Then ensues a series of prayer services: one held immediately for mourners from all denominations, followed by smaller, private memorials. Lastly evolves the sad accounting of the people lost and the terrible stories of despairing families attempting to restructure destroyed lives.

In the Atlanta of 1962, an era and city not given to public displays of emotion, recovery meant forgetting. Numerous survivors—especially those who were children at the time—told me they never talked about their lost mother, father, sister, grandmother. They were advised to go on with their daily activities as usual, as if those days would ever be "usual" again. In October 2000, television producer Chris Moser and I organized a meeting of all the Orly relatives we could locate. Our purpose was to further our research, but that gathering turned out to have a more meaningful purpose. We soon realized that this was the first time in thirty-eight years the children and close kin of those killed at Orly had held a mutual conversation about the tragedy. When the five-hour get-together ended, we were all emotionally drained but psychologically fulfilled.

From these touching and rewarding memories, I have written about the Orly tragedy that haunts me at the time when the worst terrorist attack in world history has happened to my country. Many parallels can be seen—the same stories of personal bereavement, many tales of the happy travelers whose lives were inexplicably ended, many memories of grieving families. All seems sadly familiar. And as in the aftermath of all unfathomable tragedies, a silver lining emerged following the Orly crash. Atlanta's symbol is a phoenix rising from the rubble of disaster—the initial reference is to the rebuilding of the city after General Sherman destroyed it in 1864. The phoenix rose again a century later, rejuvenating Atlanta's burned-out cultural life. From the rubble of disaster came the impetus to donate long-needed dollars for an arts center that would house a museum, art school, symphony, and theater. Today Atlanta is without question the cultural leader of the Southeast, a success accelerated because 130 people lost their lives at Orly. We can only pray that in future years, our nation will find similar positive goals as it rises from the depths of the September 11 disaster.

While the magnitude of the deaths, the loss of lives and the lasting impact on the nation in 2001 are not comparable to the 1962 disaster, there is one unmistakable reality. The final reckoning of each catastrophe is the loss of human lives, each one precious, each one irreplaceable. This is the story of those lives lost at Orly, their contributions to the city, and their legacies. It is also a glimpse back in time, to an era long forgotten, and to a disaster that devastated and transformed a major American community. From it, I hope lessons will emerge for coping with our most recent catastrophe.

Ann Uhry Abrams
Atlanta, Georgia
September 2001

Atlanta at the Crossroads

CHAPTER 1

Culture of the Capital

The European tour left Atlanta on May 9, 1962, when the Georgia capital was bursting into bloom. Magnolia buds were waiting to pop open; oaks and poplars had suddenly adorned halos of new green. Yet the memory of spring lingered in the dewy mornings and cool evenings. The inner-city was still a sleepy urban center that resembled an overgrown Southern town. Most businessmen, bankers, lawyers, and doctors had offices within two or three miles of the Five Points intersection that marked the city's center. For lunch, the men would wander over to Herren's Restaurant; their wives, out of loyalty, might meet friends at the old Frances Virginia Tea Room, a fading vestige of a more genteel past. Known for its old-fashioned, home-style cuisine, the Atlanta landmark was a favorite luncheon spot for the ladies in felt hats and white gloves.

The nation also appeared to be drenched in a long, luxurious spring. John F. Kennedy, now in office for more than a year, looked young and energetic as he vowed to initiate a New Frontier. Even those who disagreed with his policies could not deny that the Kennedy administration created a charged atmosphere of expectation, partly because the White House was injecting new energies into the arts. Jackie Kennedy was bringing music and painting into their new home, and the first couple appeared dedicated to elevating the nation's cultural awareness.

Atlanta was also on a cultural high as it prepared to welcome the Metropolitan Opera to the Fox Theater for its annual visit. The '62 season was featuring Dorothy Kirsten in *The Girl of the Golden West*, Richard Tucker in *Tosca*, and Roberta Peters in *Elektra*. Old favorites—*Lucia de Lammermoor, Aida*, and *Cossi Fan Tutte*—were also offered during the week-long festival, which ran from April 30 until May 5. Wearing newly purchased gowns, Atlanta's socially prominent women attended performances escorted by their husbands in white-jacketed summer tuxedos. During intermission they would sip cocktails at private parties across the street at the Georgian Terrace. Quite often the husbands didn't bother to go back for the second act, because opera (and all music and art, for that matter) was deemed beneath the dignity of full-blooded Southern males. After the final curtain, couples would drift off to more elaborate balls at one of the fashionable country clubs.

For some, opera week was not just cocktails and dancing. It was an oasis of culture in an otherwise airy desert. Initiated in 1910—with a short hiatus during the '30s—the glittery Met performances were the most dependable artistic professionalism the city was likely to experience at that time. Although Atlanta had a symphony, an art museum, a sprinkling of little theaters, and a well-respected ballet company, these were small, amateurish, money-starved operations held together by a coterie of enthusiastic (usually female) volunteers.

The most prominent of these, the Atlanta Symphony, had come a long way under the seemingly tireless leadership of its conductor, Henry Sopkin. By adding experienced musicians, creating a more challenging repertoire, and establishing a board of directors, he transformed a youth orchestra into a semi-professional symphony in less than two decades. Sopkin's most pressing problem was the absence of a proper venue for concerts. For its first decade, the symphony performed at the cavernous Municipal Auditorium, a 5,000 seat hall that hosted everything from the Ringling Brothers Circus to Holiday on Ice. Despite terrible acoustics and impossible working conditions, Sopkin continued to aspire toward professionalism, enlisting such stars as Risë Stevens, Jan Peerce, and Isaac Stern as guest performers. In 1958, things seemed to be improving when the symphony moved to the Tower Theater, a former movie house on Peachtree near Ponce de Leon Avenue. But in early '62, the owner of the Tower decided to use his facility for something more profitable, thus forcing the symphony back to the Auditorium for the '62-'63 season.

Similar problems plagued the sprinkling of local theaters (including Theatre Atlanta, Academy Theater, and the Pocket Theater), all of which had no permanent homes and were struggling to make ends meet. The Atlanta Ballet, one of the city's oldest performance groups, was also searching for a venue. Several possibilities to assist the performing arts were under consideration in the spring of 1962, but none carried a firm commitment.

When compared with American cities of similar size, Atlanta appeared culturally vacant. To dispel this image and obtain a first-hand glimpse of the world's masterpieces, a number of Atlantans—along with a few friends and family from out of town—were departing on May 9 for a tour of Europe. The trip was carefully scheduled to begin four days after the conclusion of opera week. That was a necessity if it were to succeed, because the social and cultural lives of a large percentage of those planning to travel revolved around the annual Met performances at the Fox Theater.

Many of the same women attending the opera and its concurrent social events were active supporters of the Atlanta Art Association, the supervising body for the High Museum and its school, formally titled the Atlanta Art Institute. The women met periodically at Women's Committee meetings, in painting classes, working together as docents, or serving in other volunteer capacities. In 1962, the institution on Peachtree was a pastiche of old houses attached to a seven-year-old brick building. A passageway from the new building led to the mansion once belonging to the J.M. High family (the original High Museum), which supplied additional gallery space. Adjoining it was the McBurney House, devoted to the decorative arts; and in back stood Thornton House, a recently reconstructed antebellum plantation residence. The art school occupied part of the High house, spreading over into the former home of the Floyd McRae family. Perhaps the most popular attraction in the entire complex was the Coach House, nestled behind the main buildings across a brick courtyard. There the Women's Committee operated a restaurant and gift shop, its profits used to keep the museum alive.

From the outset the museum had depended upon women for its sustenance. In 1905, nine of them founded a society called the "Atlanta Art Association" in hopes of promoting the fine arts in a city more attuned to making money than appreciating paintings. By then the Georgia capital was a thriving commercial center where more than 90,000 inhabitants lived and worked in a variety of enterprises ranging from banking to manufacturing. Although the young city was booming financially, it lagged behind older metropolises in collecting and exhibiting the visual arts. New York's Metropolitan Museum, for example, was already more than a quarter-century old by 1905, and New Yorkers had been amassing paintings for more than one-hundred years. Boston, Washington, Chicago, and Cincinnati all had major patrons buying artwork and helping found public museums to display it. Even Charleston, Savannah, New Orleans, and Louisville had collections of paintings and drawings hanging in private homes and art galleries. Atlantans built large mansions and filled them with fine furniture, porcelain, and crystal. But few bothered to purchase original works of art.

The nine women establishing the Art Association in 1905 vowed to introduce small exhibitions, lectures, and art classes to their materialistic hometown. Their goal was to eventually establish a museum, but they could muster neither interest nor money in the community. The city woke up slightly in 1924 when its leading furniture retailer, James Joseph Haverty, exhibited his collection of old European masters and contemporary American artists at the newly opened Biltmore Hotel. Haverty had purchased his paintings from New York's Grand Central Gallery, offering that vendor the opportunity to sell its works to wealthy Atlantans. The Grand Central exhibition of 1924 and its successor the following year captured the attention of people who had never thought seriously about the fine arts.

One of these was Hattie High, widow of the department store owner Joseph Madison High and an enthusiastic "Daughter" of the American Revolution and the Confederacy. After the second Grand Central exhibition, she offered the Atlanta Art Association her home on Peachtree at Fifteenth Street for a token purchase price of $10. In June 1926, the Tudor mansion opened as the High Museum and four months later became the setting for the third Grand Central show. For the next few years, a variety of exhibitions filled the lower floor of the High mansion while the bedrooms above provided space for art classes. Sometimes

Atlantans loaned works to the museum from their homes and occasionally New York galleries exhibited artwork. The guiding force during the late '20s and '30s was a board of directors selected from Atlanta's leading businessmen, headed by J.J. Haverty with a great deal of financial support from Walter Hill, president of the Retail Credit Corporation. Funds were always scarce, but donations from board members managed to sustain the museum and school through the Depression.

In the early '40s, the wife of banker Thomas Glenn gave $35,000 to construct an additional gallery called "Memory Lane," named to reflect the sentiments of a poem by Maurice Maeterlinck. The gallery was reserved as a place for paintings contributed in memory of loved ones. In making the bequest, Mrs. Glenn stipulated that no "harsh, unpleasant, unhappy, morbid, or controversial" subjects be hung in the gallery and insisted that the museum accept only works by painters who had "been dead for more than thirty years." As a result of these restrictions, Memory Lane contained a conglomeration of traditional artworks, some of questionable attribution and quality. But an inadequately-funded institution could not afford to be picky, and the Atlanta Art Association wanted badly to fill its walls.

At the end of World War II, the permanent collection of the museum was a scattershot amalgamation of donations ranging from dusted-off attic contents to new works by local artists. The quality improved in 1949 when the Haverty family presented thirty works from J.J. Haverty's collection, including paintings by Mary Cassatt, John Henry Twachtman, Henry O. Tanner, and John Singer Sargent. They were hung in an additional house, purchased for the museum by Henry B. Scott. In the early 1950s, the Kress Foundation offered a number of Renaissance and Baroque paintings if the Atlanta Art Association would construct a fire-proof building with proper climate controls. A fundraising drive produced $675,000 for a red-brick and glass structure which opened in 1955. In that same year the museum acquired the house next door, left as a bequest by its former occupant, E.P. McBurney. In his will, McBurney stipulated that his home be used only to display decorative arts. In 1961, the association added a reconstructed antebellum plantation house to the premises, thereby increasing the number of buildings, most connected by passageways.

At the rear of the McBurney home sat a detached carriage house. Shortly after the Atlanta Art Association took over the property in 1955, a newly formed Women's Committee began rebuilding the old structure and converting it into a tearoom and gift shop. The Coach House restaurant "was the 'in' place to go to lunch," commented *Atlanta Journal* society writer Edith Hills Coogler. "Merely to eat there amounted to an introduction to Atlanta Society, not that many charwomen put this to the test. It was operated by the local nobility."

The "nobility" that comprised the museum's Women's Committee had prestige well before it started operating the Coach House. When it began in 1955, the organization had already attracted more than 500 members. From flea markets held on the museum lawn to its "Browse, Borrow and Buy" gallery run by the indomitable Sylvia Ferst, the women were in charge. They had clout because they produced not only funds but community interest. A large part of the Coach House's success came from its elitist reputation.

Many of the so-called "Coach House Ladies" began working at the museum to fulfill their Junior League volunteer requirements. Their sole purpose was to raise money for the museum by sponsoring exhibitions, auctions, flea markets, flower arranging competitions, and opening its quarters for social functions that ranged from garden club luncheons to debutante parties. By 1961, the Women's Committee was firmly entrenched as the institution's most powerful fund raiser, therefore wielding great influence with the staff and board of trustees.

Their auction in the fall of 1960 hatched the Art Association's European tour. The catalyst was the new Air France district manager, Paul Dossans, who had come to Atlanta in 1959 to establish the airline's presence in the Southeast. In pursuit of that objective, the innovative Dossans began making contacts and devising public relations schemes, one of which was offering a free trip to Paris as a prize at the Art Association auction. The Frenchman was the epitome of Gallic magnetism, with his suave good looks and debonair manner. The publicity surrounding the auction gift worked so well that Dossans decided to try again. While meeting with volunteers before the 1960 auction, he encountered Anne Merritt, an active member of the Women's Committee. As they talked, he learned that this attractive, well-dressed Atlantan loved to travel. In fact, she often organized European tours under the auspices of American Express. In Anne Merritt, Dossans saw a golden opportunity. Why not combine forces to offer a chartered Air France flight to Paris in conjunction with an American Express tour of Europe?

When Dossans asked Anne Merritt to spearhead the tour, she realized it would be a perfect project for the Women's Committee. Not only could the Art Association benefit by requiring all participants to become museum members, but it would also provide an inexpensive vacation for the organization's supporters and volunteers. They therefore struck a deal. Merritt agreed to arrange the trip if she could obtain free passage for herself and her friend Joan (pronounced Jo-Ann) Self from the small town of Marks, Mississippi. Having discovered each other through their husbands' business connections, the two women often toured Europe together. Before jet-travel, they journeyed aboard prop planes, which involved several stopovers and at least twenty-four hours in transit.

Born in 1920, Anne Garrett Merritt grew up in Druid Hills— the eldest daughter of Lillian and Dr. Steven Arthur Garrett, a prominent Atlanta dentist. After skipping a couple of grades, she finished high school at age sixteen and enrolled in Mt. Vernon Junior College in Washington. However, when her mother became ill with tuberculosis, Anne returned home to help care for her father and younger sister, Susan, while continuing her education at Agnes Scott College in nearby Decatur. After her mother's death, Anne transferred to the University of Georgia in Athens and there met her future husband, William Merritt. They married in 1942, shortly after she graduated from Georgia and he finished at Harvard Business School. During World War II, the Merritts lived in Washington, while William served as an Army lieutenant stationed at the Pentagon.

Afterwards they returned to Atlanta to raise their three children, William Jr., Anne, and Martha (Marti) in a house on Peachtree Battle Avenue. William Merritt ran the regional office of H.J. Baker & Brothers, an agricultural chemical brokerage based in Connecticut, while Anne stayed busy teaching Sunday school at St. Phillips Episcopal Cathedral, studying the fine arts, cooking gourmet meals, and entertaining. When Anne Merritt wasn't traveling herself, she was escorting wives of convention delegates to current exhibitions at the museum followed by tea or luncheon at the Coach House. All profits accrued to the Art Association. A good-looking, self assured woman, Anne Merritt loved showing off her figure and boasting about the whistles that came from passing men. But despite her sexy femininity, Merritt was tough. According to her son: "Nobody—and I mean NOBODY—wanted to cross swords with her a second time."

This steel edge served her well when she negotiated costs with American Express and Air France. And it also benefited the Art Association.

Shortly after she and Dossans began plans for the European tour, Anne Merritt decided to recruit Lydia Black as an assistant. She was aware that Lydia had a wide circle of acquaintances and was a whiz at accomplishing things, so Anne promised Lydia a free trip if she would help with recruiting. Born in 1917 as the third child of Caspar and Mary Whitner, she and her sister, Cornelia, who was less than two years her junior, were inseparable companions. Friends remembered them as a beautiful and happy pair with keen senses of humor.

After finishing at North Fulton High School, Lydia Whitner enrolled in Agnes Scott and soon began dating an Emory student named David Black. He, too, had grown up in Atlanta and they ran around with the same crowd. In 1940, a year after he earned his law degree and she graduated from Agnes Scott, they married. For a short while the newlyweds lived in Birmingham, Alabama, where he was general manager of Southern Airways; but in 1942, David Black—like most young men of his generation—entered the armed services. At the war's end, David returned to Atlanta to become the assistant secretary of the Trust Company of Georgia, one of the city's leading banks, and Lydia poured her talents into volunteer work.

A mover and shaker in social and cultural circles, Lydia Black was president of both the Junior League and Cherokee Garden Club and an active participant in numerous other charitable organizations. In other words, this trim, chic, and polished brunette had the kind of charisma that not only drew people within her orbit, but succeeded in commanding attention in all endeavors she pursued. She and Anne Merritt shared a great deal. They were close in age, grew up in Atlanta, both attended Agnes

Scott, belonged to the Junior League, and traveled in the same social milieu. Together they could attract an interesting group of Atlantans to journey abroad.

The first person they spoke with was Women's Committee chairman, Ruth McMillan. Since her retirement two years earlier as executive secretary for the regional vice-president of Sears, Ruth devoted all of her energies to volunteer work. In fact, while she was still at Sears, charities—ranging from the First Methodist Church to the Atlanta Symphony and Egleston Children's Hospital—occupied most of her free time. The eclectic mix of her interests defined her complex and munificent character. Never married, she lived quietly on Beverly Road with her older sister, Mae. Newscaster Aubrey Morris rented a room from the McMillan sisters shortly after he arrived in Atlanta in the late 1940s to be a cub reporter for the *Atlanta Journal*. He remembered Ruth as a "cultured effervescent lady but very businesslike. She had no affectations, no pretenses," he recalled, "and most of all maintained a genuine interest in Atlanta and its cultural life."

Early in her professional career, the petite and sparkly innovator had served as a secretary for Harry Hopkins, one of President Franklin Roosevelt's top advisors, then manager of the Red Cross's Atlanta Division. Wearing her "civic" hat, Ruth McMillan was very active in the Southeastern Regional Conference of Women in Chambers of Commerce. Atlanta had already recognized Ruth's talents when they named her "Woman of the Year in Civic Affairs" in 1955, a mark of distinction in those days. Begun in 1943, and continuing for twenty-nine years, the WOTY committee annually honored women who distinguished themselves through extraordinary service in business, the arts, civic affairs, education, and the professions. Three other women who signed up for the Art Association tour (Raiford Ragsdale,

Rosalind Williams, and Katherine Bleckley) received that award
and two others (Julia Jones and Lydia Black) chaired the WOTY
board of directors.

Ruth McMillan felt the full weight of her responsibility as
chairman of the Art Association's Women's Committee. She
once complained to Board of Trustees president, Del Paige, that
all committees should be opened to anyone who wished to participate, because she feared some of the women were treating
the museum as if it were an exclusive social club. It also worried
her that many trustees had not joined the parent organization.
Not only was it wrong to be involved in policy-making without
having their names on the membership list, but their dues
would add needed dollars to the museum's treasury.

Ruth McMillan's distress with the Atlanta Art Association
points to the inefficiency and mismanagement that plagued the
institution. Its paid staff consisted of Reginald Poland, Director
of the High Museum; James Nonemaker, Decorative Arts Curator;
Guthrie Foster, administrator of the art school; a treasurer, a few
secretaries, and a small maintenance staff. Poland, Nonemaker,
and Foster each had complete authority over his or her domain,
and each depended on volunteers—especially Women's Committee
members—to raise money and perform duties of day-to-day
operation.

Sixty-nine-year-old Reginald Poland—who held degrees
from Brown, Princeton, and Harvard—came to Atlanta in 1951
after a long career in museum administration in Denver, Detroit,
West Palm Beach, and San Diego, where he was Director of the
Museum of Fine Arts. Hawk-nosed and gaunt, Poland was a
bundle of nervous energy that served him well during his first
few years at the High Museum. Not only was he largely instrumental in obtaining the Kress Collection, but he also spear-

headed construction of the new building and orchestrated several ambitious exhibitions. In fact, during his administration, the High Museum was beginning to aspire toward professionalism. But by the end of 1961, Poland seemed incapable of keeping the institution out of debt and powerless to prevent the volunteers from establishing policy for everything from grounds maintenance to art acquisition.

Poland's counterpart at the art school, Elizabeth Guthrie Foster, was in many ways his antithesis. In her quiet and professional manner, the prim and low-keyed artist—whose specialty was working with fabrics—took charge of her duties with self-assurance. When she came to Atlanta in 1958 from the University of Alabama, the forty-five-year-old artist found the buildings in serious disrepair and the staff demoralized. Only a few years earlier, the school had almost been forced to close and was saved at the eleventh hour by a successful fundraising effort spurred by Atlanta executive James V. Carmichael and a team of devoted volunteers. After raising $90,000 to rescue the school from near destruction, the committee realized it had to restructure the entire operation. Guthrie Foster therefore had a daunting task before her.

Her first effort went toward having the school accredited by the Southern Association of Colleges and Schools. That accomplished, she endeavored to boost enrollment and help top students get accepted in graduate art programs. For her achievements, Guthrie Foster won Atlanta's Woman of the Year award for 1960. By 1962, the school was back on its feet and under Foster's direction was striving for excellence. But the buildings were still falling down, and the art school had a long way to go to match similar institutions in other cities. To put it bluntly: help was desperately needed.

That assistance required the approval of the seventy-three-person Art Association Board of Trustees, led by its chairman, James Carmichael, and president, Delbert Paige. Carmichael was a Renaissance man, whose accomplishments ranged from law and politics to business and the arts, all pursued with clear-headed dedication. Although physically handicapped from a youthful accident, his energy never lagged. During World War II, he began his Atlanta career by running the Bell Bomber plant in Marietta. Recipient of a law degree and a former member of the Georgia General Assembly, Carmichael ran for Georgia governor in 1946, winning the popular vote but losing to Herman Talmadge because of the antiquated county-unit system that gave rural counties control of state elections. In the early '60s, Carmichael became president of Scripto, an Atlanta-based pen and pencil manufacturer. He had played a leading role in rescuing the school when it was threatened with extinction during the mid-fifties, and his loyalty to that institution would play a key role in changing Atlanta's arts scene.

In 1962, however, the position of Art Association board chairman was largely that of overseer. The responsibility for running the complicated structure of the disjointed organization fell on the shoulders of the president. In that position, the tall, kindly, gregarious Del Paige—a resident partner in the international accounting firm of Ernst & Ernst—took his charge seriously. From his arrival in Atlanta in 1930, he rapidly gained respect as one of the city's most prominent civic and cultural activists. Everyone who worked with Del Paige admired his sincere commitment to each organization he served and praised the relaxed, gentle manner in which he handled complex problems. His wife Winifred often worked alongside him, especially at the museum where she was an active member of the Women's Committee. The Paiges had no children, so volunteering seemed to channel their energies and their income into productive ways to help their city.

When Del Paige took over as board president in 1960, his major concern was the disastrous state of the organization's finances. From his long experience in accounting, he was well aware that management of the Art Association was in serious disarray and he was determined to get the institution on a more secure footing. Thus when trustee and executive committee member Laura Dorsey (a sister of Lydia Black) came to him in early 1961 suggesting a professional survey of the association, Paige readily agreed. Her primary interest was the school, which she believed was being treated poorly by the parent organization. At her urging, Paige presented the idea of a thorough investigation to the board and gave Dorsey the task of seeking money to fund it. She succeeded in raising the bulk of it from the J. Bulow Campbell Foundation and the Junior League.

By the fall of '61, the board had approved the consulting firm of Engelhardt, Engelhardt and Leggett to conduct the survey. Three men—Richard B.K. McLanathan, curator of Decorative Arts and Secretary of the Museum of Fine Arts in Boston; Wilhelmus B. Bryan, Director of the Minneapolis School of Art; and Richard Franco Goldman, author, composer, art critic, and former professor at the Julliard School of Music—were assigned to scrutinize the various components of the Atlanta Art Association. The entire investigating process and its ensuing published report would take place over the course of the next six to eight months.

Just about the time the trustees agreed to proceed with the Engelhardt study, Ruth McMillan revealed a "secret" to the Atlanta Art Association's board. The setting was their October 18, 1961 meeting in the glass-fronted member's room on the museum's ground floor. She began by saying that rumors were flying, so she might as well confess. The "energetic" Women's Committee was hoping to sponsor a deluxe "trip to the Louvre" the following May that would "make money" in a "charming (legal) way." The clincher, she said, was that applicants must be museum members for at least six months before departure in order to be eligible.

The Women's Committee accepted the news with enthusiasm and authorized Anne Merritt and Lydia Black to reserve a chartered jet that would hold 140 people. To spur enrollment, American Express produced a colorful brochure. "Your trip will be carefree and unforgettable," the booklet asserted. The first mailing also contained a letter from Del Paige. "This is your chance of a lifetime," he began. The price tag of only $895 for the full tour was indeed a "fantastic bargain" when compared with the standard first-class jet fare of $1,072.82. It included an escorted excursion, beginning in Paris and proceeding to London, Amsterdam, Lucerne, Venice, Florence, Rome, and returning for a four day stay in the French capital. For those choosing to travel independently, a round trip ticket aboard the chartered jet would cost only $388, a bargain compared to the standard economy fare of $631.64. And for everyone aboard the plane, the first night at Paris's Hôtel du Louvre was free.

Del and Winifred Paige were among the first to sign up; and because of her role in promoting the trip, Ruth McMillan also agreed to go along. With these top museum volunteers on board, Lydia Black and Anne Merritt began a campaign to recruit friends, neighbors, and family. By January 1962, they had a list of eighty-six names, many of whom had remitted the requisite $250 deposit. There were still approximately fifty vacancies and given the expected attrition rate, they clearly needed to find more travelers. If they failed to enlist the minimum amount to make it profitable for Air France, the fares would have to be higher.

On February 4, 1962, the Women's Committee presented a preview of the trip in the Art Association's Walter Hill Auditorium. Hixon Kinsella, a prominent advertising executive and amateur photographer, showed slides of the places to be visited accompanied by music to set the mood. A few days later, columnist Margaret Turner—who was also considering going with the group—wrote an article about the proposed tour and pictured Winifred Paige, Ruth McMillan, and Lydia Black holding maps, booklets, and a passport. By March the chartered flight was still short forty people, not enough to reach the desired "comfortable margin." Throughout the month, the Women's Committee contacted museum trustees and members in hopes of persuading them to participate. As further inducement, Anne Merritt invited those who were considering the trip to a coffee at her home on Peachtree Battle Avenue.

Minutes of the Art Association board meetings reveal that the most pressing problem facing the institution in early 1962 was neither the shortage of passengers for the "Trip to the Louvre" nor the ongoing Engelhardt investigation. Rather, it was the precarious financial state of the museum and the school. The Art Association was decidedly in the red, although once again generous donors promised to rescue the failing museum and school. At the January 1962 meeting of the executive committee, acting secretary Harold Patterson announced that Dr. Reginald Poland was planning to retire. With this surprising information on the table, the Engelhardt investigators began interviewing staff and board members for their study.

As the three-man committee probed around during February 1962, the museum opened a major exhibition entitled "Landscape Into Art." The three-week show, partly sponsored by the Women's Committee, included over ninety paintings, illuminated manuscripts, and tapestries borrowed from museums around the country and Europe. Despite the unprecedented appearance in Atlanta of noted European artworks, the exhibition received only scant mention in the local newspapers. But even with scant publicity, the museum cleared $2,300 from the opening party and door receipts.

In March, the Engelhardt team completed its study and issued a report. The appraisal was direct and critical, although not entirely surprising. With the exception of the "main museum" constructed in 1955, the study condemned the conglomerate of "non-fire-resistive" old buildings. Among the many recommendations for modernizing the association, the committee suggested that the Association sponsor a "Friends" committee with male and female members to replace the Women's Committee.

The investigators were equally as disapproving of the organizational structure. They criticized the seventy-three person Board of Trustees as being too large and advised that it be reduced to approximately twenty people, with an even smaller executive committee. The report concluded that because the art museum, decorative arts museum, and school operated "with little reference to each other," the result was "chaos and disorganization." In general, however, the study praised the school for accomplishing so much "under adverse or primitive conditions" and recommended that it receive a more equitable share of the Association's funding. The board was scheduled to discuss the Engelhardt Report during its April meeting and decide whether or not to accept it in May, just before the European tour departed.

Meanwhile Del Paige—in a different role—was deeply involved in another arts-related project. In 1960, Mayor William B. Hartsfield had appointed him along with thirteen other prominent citizens to a "Cultural Needs Committee" assigned to study what the city required to improve its performing arts facilities. The group chose Paige to chair the investigation that hoped to come up with a proposal in early May of 1962. Clearly the city was on the threshold of major cultural changes as the

Atlanta Art Association prepared to go abroad. It was an exciting time to be involved in the arts even though the challenges were immense.

Only weeks before the scheduled May 9 departure, all decisions seemed to be suspended. Del Paige and other interested participants faced Atlanta's cultural future with a mixture of optimism and anxiety. Although acceptance of the Engelhardt study remained uncertain and the city's "Cultural Needs Committee" was still considering plans for a performing arts center, there was one program that was close to achieving its goals. On April 10, Anne Merritt told the Women's Committee that more than 110 people had signed up for the "Trip to the Louvre." They only needed a few more reservations to meet Air France's requirement.

CHAPTER 2

❧ The City Too Busy to Hate

Raiford Ragsdale was actually older than most others who signed up for the Atlanta Arts Association tour, even though her drive and enthusiasm matched that of a much younger woman. This energy accompanied a sense of Southern propriety that kept part of her firmly rooted in the past. For decades her life had been intertwined with the city of her birth. Not only had she been chosen in 1951 as the Woman of the Year in the Arts, but she had earned numerous distinctions as a political, educational, and charitable leader. Her diverse career epitomized the dynamic complexities of a city balanced between Southern dignity and self-aggrandizing ambition. In 1898, when Raiford was four years old, her father, Stephen Price Moncrief, patented a furnace and founded a company to distribute his new product. Because central heating was relatively new in the late nineteenth century, he was a pioneer in the field. Within two decades, Moncrief Furnaces heated homes across the Southeast; and the former son of a Gwinett County farmer was propelled into moderate prosperity.

Raiford—the eldest of Moncrief's five daughters and one son—lived comfortably with her family on Cleburne Avenue in Inman Park and later on Lullwater Road in Druid Hills. She grew up to be a beautiful woman, reasonably tall, with dark hair and eyes, and conveyed a sense of dignity and graciousness. At Bessie Tift, a Baptist women's college in Forsythe, Georgia, Raiford studied music and drama, appearing frequently in pageants, plays, and glee club concerts and pouring herself into extra-curricular activities. For unknown reasons, after her junior year, she transferred to Brenau College in Gainesville, Georgia, and graduated from there around 1916.

While on vacation from college, she met Clifford Ragsdale, the son of a successful livestock dealer whose family had a rags-to-moderate-riches background similar to the Moncriefs. Twelve years her senior, Cliff was a craggy-faced, blue-eyed outdoorsman, who worked with his father in one of the largest distributors of livestock in the United States. They married in May 1920, and while Cliff traveled around the nation selling cattle, mules, and horses, Raiford stayed home to take care of their daughter, born in 1924. But after a few years of domesticity, she knew she was not content to play bridge and be a hostess, although women of means and social ambition rarely entered the workplace in those days. She would have to find another way to fulfill her ambition.

That happened in 1926 when her father-in-law, Isaac Newton Ragsdale, was elected mayor of Atlanta. A highlight of his four-year tenure came when Charles Lindbergh visited Atlanta in October 1927, a scarce five months after his historic flight across the Atlantic. Mayor Ragsdale was at Candler Field, a small airstrip south of town, when The Spirit of St. Louis landed, and he escorted the national hero to several events staged by the city. By his side were members of his family, including several of his daughters and his only son, Clifford, with his wife, Raiford, who watched and learned. It was an excellent education.

During his mayoralty, I.N. Ragsdale built schools, improved city parks, and expanded the city limits to incorporate fledgling suburban neighborhoods. He also engineered the city's purchase of Candler Field and embarked on an airport extension. When Ragsdale left the mayor's office in 1931, his administration had weathered the beginnings of the Depression and a scandal that convicted fifteen city officials of graft. Acquitted of compliance in the payoffs, the mayor could be satisfied that he had presided over a period of record growth. Seven years later, William B. Hartsfield became mayor and established himself in City Hall for almost a quarter century, with only one brief hiatus in the early '40s.

In 1942, Atlanta's population stood at 503,000, almost double the number of residents in 1930. Part of that growth spurt was due to the Second World War. Even before the United States officially joined the fight, Atlanta—a key railroad center during the Civil War—found itself once more a transportation hub. Railroad cars filled with servicemen rolled continually through Terminal, Union, and Brookwood Stations bringing recruits to military training bases throughout Georgia.

The war offered Raiford Ragsdale a way to exhibit her executive abilities. Beginning as a low-rank volunteer with the Red Cross, she soon became chairwoman of the Fulton County Women's Division and deputy director of the bureau that distributed gifts, food, and clothing to the state's military bases and hospitals. Her astute eye for publicity meant that her picture appeared often in the newspapers. Strikingly handsome in her Red Cross uniform, she was photographed alone or with groups of volunteers.

These wartime executive posts whetted Raiford's appetite for organizational work, and when peace came she agreed to head the Women's Division of the Georgia Democratic Party. Her quest for publicity meant she was often pictured as a spokesperson for various local candidates. In the late '40s, she became a volunteer leader of the Atlanta Symphony and the Atlanta Music Club. For those efforts, she was chosen Woman of the Year in the Arts in 1951. It was obvious to all who knew her: Raiford Ragsdale was primed to forge ahead.

Her opportunity arose when the Eighth Ward representative on the Atlanta Board of Education resigned in 1953. Raiford decided to run to become the first woman to fill that post. With her reputation as a capable and determined achiever, Raiford campaigned hard all summer but always tempered her political savvy with comments about her domestic capabilities and comments on fashion. That approach paid off and she amassed more votes than the sum total of her three male opponents. No one doubted that Raiford Ragsdale would turn her untiring managerial skills toward energizing the Board of Education, just as she had done in every activity she touched. Not only did she initiate a science program and push to raise teachers' salaries, she never missed a graduation at any of the city's twenty-three high schools. In the '50s that meant visiting both white and "colored" schools, a moderately bold move in the strongly segregated city.

Yet Raiford was not a liberal as younger generations understand the term. Conformity and social acceptance were far too important to her. While she focused attention on improving the quality of education in Atlanta, the city was crossing a new barrier. Throughout his mayoral reign, Hartsfield had success-fully engineered a coalition of white, well-off, and worldly busi-ness leaders to help facilitate his projects. His power structure included his old friend Robert W. Woodruff, chairman of Coca-Cola; John Sibley, chairman of the Trust Company of Georgia; Mills Lane, chairman of the Citizens and Southern Bank; and Ivan Allen Jr., president of an office-supply company and chair-man of the Atlanta Chamber of Commerce.

By the mid '50s, they were facing an unprecedented chal-lenge. An impressive array of black leaders—headed by John Wesley Dobbs, Reverend William Holmes Borders, and A. T. Walden—were demanding an end to the half-century-old Jim Crow laws that froze the African American community into a subservient role. Although the majority of white Atlantans took Jim Crow restrictions for granted, the wall of white compla-cency was beginning to crumble. In 1953, the same voters who placed Raiford Ragsdale on the Board of Education also chose Dr. Rufus Clement, the distinguished president of Atlanta University, to be the first African American to serve in that body. A year after that election, the U. S. Supreme Court issued its edict in favor of school desegregation in the landmark case, Brown v. Board of Education.

Like most white Southerners, Atlanta mayor William Hartsfield voiced a firm belief in maintaining the status quo. But as an astute politician, he also realized he could not ignore increasing pressures from the black community. The last thing he needed was a riot. Therefore during the late '50s, the mayor and members of the city's white power structure met frequently with African American leaders to determine peaceful paths toward eventual integration. Hartsfield's nemesis was Georgia Governor Marvin Griffin, a loud and rabid segregationist, who was devis-ing schemes to stave off integration. Aware that angry resistance to the Supreme Court's rulings could diversely affect Atlanta's image, Hartsfield found ways to outmaneuver Griffin, one being the smooth desegregation of Atlanta's parks.

But school integration posed a more challenging dilemma, and Griffin and his White Citizens' Council cohorts vowed loudly to stop it at all costs. This growing racial tension spilled over into the election of May 1957, producing a close call for Raiford Ragsdale, who defeated her male opponent by only 411 votes. But her problems were miniscule compared to Hartsfield's. He had barely squeaked by in the last election and realized that his hold over the electorate was precariously shaky as he embarked on his sixth term. His nightmares seemed to materialize in October 1958, when the religious school of The Temple, home of Atlanta's oldest and then-only Reformed Jewish Congregation, was ripped apart by forty sticks of dynamite.

It was one of many such bombings of Sunday schools and churches throughout the South. But it was the first such occurrence in Atlanta. Although no one was hurt, the incident received national publicity because it happened at a critical juncture of Atlanta's attempt to integrate peacefully. Not only was it an overt act of anti-Semitism, but the bombing was linked to the Civil Rights movement because the Temple's rabbi, Jacob M. Rothschild, was an outspoken advocate of desegregation.

As 1958 advanced, the process of integration began to accelerate. In March, two influential black American ministers representing two generations—the greatly revered Reverend William Holmes Borders and a young activist named Martin Luther King Jr.—led a boycott of black clergymen aboard Atlanta busses and demanded seats in the front. Under orders from police chief Herbert Jenkins, they were arrested but immediately released on bond. The case went before the Federal Court which declared the Jim Crow seating illegal and Atlanta's busses were summarily integrated.

In her final two years on the Board of Education, Raiford Ragsdale and her fellow board members faced one of the greatest challenges in the city's history: how would they comply with the Brown decision? In June 1959, U.S. District Judge Frank A. Hooper ruled that the city must come up with a plan for school integration and implement it in "a reasonable time." While the controversy surrounding desegregation simmered, Georgia elected Lieutenant Governor Ernest Vandiver to succeed Griffin as governor. The mild-mannered, forty-year-old lawyer was more moderate on racial issues than his rabble-rousing predecessor. Yet in order to win the state-wide election, Vandiver vowed that while he was governor no black child would attend a white school. He was soon to eat those words.

Under a scheme devised by his chief of staff, Griffin Bell, Vandiver formed a commission directed by retired bank president and well-respected moderate, John A. Sibley. Its purpose was to hold hearings throughout the state with the ostensible purpose of feeling the public pulse. Those testifying before his panel would be presented with the either-or question: should the state allow limited integration or should there be no schools at all? In the long run, he was able to put down the white supremacist hecklers and report to the state legislature that Georgians would accept integration rather than destroy their public school system.

Shortly before the Sibley Commission held its hearings, Atlanta discovered a more dynamic catalyst for ending segregation. In January 1960, Dr. Martin Luther King Jr. moved the headquarters of his Southern Christian Leadership Conference

(SCLC) to his home town. Having grown up in Atlanta as the son and namesake of one of the city's most prominent black ministers, King realized that the thriving metropolis with its vibrant black American university community was the perfect place to anchor his civil rights campaign.

To mark King's arrival in March 1960, Atlanta University students were gearing up for a non-violent confrontation. Their target was the city's segregated lunch counters. Led by Julian Bond, Lonnie King, and other members of the newly-formed Student Nonviolent Coordinating Committee (SNCC), young blacks began a series of sit-ins at lunch counters, only to be forcefully removed by the police, who carried out their duties without raising a club. The student campaign came to a head in October 1960, when a band of well-dressed black college students tried to enter Rich's Magnolia Room. With them was Martin Luther King Jr., who had heretofore not participated in the sit-ins.

When the protesters refused to leave, the police handcuffed thirty-five students along with their prominent leader and ushered them away. By refusing the $500 bond, King spent the first night of his life in prison. A few days following the arrest, accelerated demonstrations by blacks threatened to alarm once-complacent white moderates, who were equally disturbed by counter demonstrations by rabid segregationists. National TV coverage filmed it all, and Mayor Hartsfield confronted the worst nightmare of his career.

After frantic negotiations, Hartsfield arranged for the students to be freed. King, however, stayed in jail because a DeKalb County judge held him on a minor traffic infraction. Before the episode ended, King was taken to Reidsville, the state's maximum security prison. It was a shocking move and one destined to backfire. The catalyst for King's release was none other than the Democratic presidential candidate, Senator John F. Kennedy, who telephoned

Coretta King to express his concern. Then another call to the DeKalb County judge from his brother, Robert, followed. In the end King was released on a $2,000 bond and as word of the Kennedy's intervention spread around the country, African Americans turned out at the polls on election day to shift the balance toward Kennedy in a dramatically close election.

In December 1960, two months after King's arrest, a decision in the case of *Holmes v. Danner* ruled that two African Americans from Atlanta, Charlayne Hunter and Hamilton Holmes, could enter the University of Georgia. To defend the students, the NAACP sent Constance Baker Motley to work with Atlanta attorneys, Horace T. Ward, Donald Hollowell, and a young clerk named Vernon Jordan. When Hunter and Holmes reached the campus on January 9, 1961, they found that the original ruling had been reversed. After rapid legal maneuverings, attorneys for the two black students—with help from Fifth Circuit Judge Elbert P. Tuttle—succeeded in overriding the reversal. Although they had to endure taunts from angry mobs, Hunter and Holmes began classes and the state's universities were technically desegregated.

It was at this point that Raiford Ragsdale decided to run for a third term on the Atlanta Board of Education. As she was mounting her campaign in the spring of '61, the school board approved a plan to integrate Atlanta's public schools starting with the twelfth grade and working downward. It was merely a token, but it satisfied the court mandate. In the coming fall term, ten carefully-screened black students were scheduled to enroll in white high schools. Even though integration was uppermost in most voters' minds, Raiford avoided the issue during her campaign. "We must provide a well-rounded program geared to meet the needs of all children," she told reporters, "the normal, the handicapped and the gifted." She never mentioned "Negroes."

Ragsdale's chief opponents were Atlanta businessman, Dan T. MacIntyre III, and a League of Women Voters activist named Sara Mitchell. Unlike Raiford, the eager and determined Mitchell was an outspoken proponent of school integration while Raiford avoided the issue entirely. On the rare occasions that Ragsdale attended a rally before a racially mixed audience, she stuck to a prescribed text about her previous accomplishments on the school board. Meanwhile Sara Mitchell was appealing directly to blacks. Speaking to the Atlanta Negro Voters League, she said: "Everyone who is satisfied with the schools the way they are [should] vote for Mrs. Ragsdale. Those who aren't . . . should vote for me."

In early September 1961, policemen lined the streets around several formerly all-white high schools. But the anticipated trouble never occurred. When white protesters became too obstreperous, the police arrested them and the black students remained in school unharmed. Hartsfield liked to proclaim that Atlanta was "a city too busy to hate," and the uneventful school desegregation proved to be his last triumph. The old war-horse was savvy enough to know it was time to get out before the racial temperature again began to rise. On June 7, 1961—a few months before he presided over the carefully orchestrated desegregation process—Hartsfield announced that he would not run again.

With the mayor retiring, the city's top post was up for grabs. Ivan Allen Jr. eyed it cautiously. For many years, he had been priming for electoral office. Encouraged by his father, a former state senator, he entered the gubernatorial race in 1957 only to withdraw when he realized that rural Georgia would never support a wealthy Atlantan. The city of his birth was a different matter. There he was the well-respected scion of a prominent family and younger member of the white power structure that made the city hum. As chairman of the high profile Chamber of

Commerce during the sit-in conflict, Ivan Allen Jr. had been involved in negotiations with African American leaders which caused him to question the traditional Southern values he had always accepted. Despite his aristocratic drawl and courtly manners, he was slowly morphing into a moderate liberal. His rationale was economic. From his vantage point as Chamber president, he knew that businesses would suffer in a city torn by racial strife.

With the guaranteed support of older black leaders and the white power structure, he stood a good chance of becoming mayor. Thus shortly after Hartsfield announced his retirement, Allen entered the race. Four formidable opponents faced him in the September 13 nonpartisan election, but it soon boiled down to a free-for-all between Allen and arch-segregationist Lester Maddox, owner of the Pickrick Restaurant, whose specialties were fried chicken, iced tea, and segregationist propaganda. Greeting customers with axe-handles to swing at aggressive "niggers," the round-faced, bespectacled Maddox played the part of a clown while spewing the venom of racism.

On election day, black voters turned out in record numbers to catapult Allen into first place with 38,000 votes; Maddox came in second with 20,000. The lines were drawn for their next confrontation in a runoff. The heavy turn-out of African Americans on September 13 worked against Raiford Ragsdale. Given the polemics between Allen and Maddox, she had hoped to win her usual support from moderate whites, but this time that strategy failed. Sara Mitchell garnered 33,325 votes; MacIntyre won 27,128; and Raiford came in a poor third with 20,199. Her proper, white-gloved demeanor and avoidance of the burning racial questions were out of step with her changing city. Suddenly she seemed every bit of her sixty-seven years. The future belonged to younger moderates.

They triumphed in the September 20 runoff when the coalition of blacks and white businessmen granted Allen sixty-four percent of the votes to make him mayor. It also gave Sara Mitchell an edge over the more conservative MacIntyre, and she was elected to fill Raiford Ragsdale's seat on the Board of Education. Quietly Raiford stepped back from public life and turned once again to the museum and the symphony, accelerating her volunteer activities. As a member of the Art Association board, she could easily justify taking her first trip to Europe as a way to serve her city. Now a widow, she was anxious to enhance her own knowledge, and after the disappointment of her defeat a scarce eight months earlier, the European excursion seemed the perfect panacea.

As she was preparing for her departure, Raiford Ragsdale may have sensed that the era of integration and leadership of Ivan Allen Jr. would differ markedly from the old days when her father-in-law—or even Bill Hartsfield—presided over the city "too busy to hate."

CHAPTER 3

≈ Society at a Crossroads

"When I moved into the mayor's office on January 2, 1962," Ivan Allen Jr. commented, "it was obvious that Atlanta and Georgia and the rest of the South had come to the crossroads; that a time of dynamic change lay ahead of us." It was at that crossroads, with Allen's term just beginning and Atlanta society undergoing jarring changes, that a number of the new mayor's close friends were signing up for a three-week trip to Europe. Some of them were among the 352 people jamming the Aldermanic Chamber to watch Allen become the city's forty-sixth mayor.

They may not have agreed with his increasingly liberal views, but political opinions mattered less than lifelong ties, and his friends—who also came from old Atlanta families—supported him with enthusiasm. He was, after all, "one of them."

Within the sealed security of their comfortable surroundings, their Atlanta was a small, compatible town where everyone knew each other. Their lives centered around the Piedmont Driving Club or Capital City Club, where they danced to the music of visiting celebrity bands at elaborate balls. Most of the women "came out" at the Driving Club at age nineteen or twenty and were presented to society on the arms of their fathers before being caught up in a whirl of luncheons, teas, and dinner parties. Afterward, they usually found husbands from other prominent families and settled into lives similar to those of their parents, joining the Junior League and volunteering for charities.

Of all those considering the Art Association tour in the spring of 1962, none had a more solid pedigree than Henrietta Collier Armstrong Ayer, whose family history follows the development of Atlanta from its beginnings. Her great-great-grandfather, Meredith Collier, migrated with his twin brother from North Carolina in 1823 at the time when Cherokees were being forced to vacate their homes to make room for white settlers. The Colliers settled in DeKalb County, which then encompassed the territory that would someday become Atlanta. There Meredith Collier farmed, raised fourteen children, manned the local post office, and served as district magistrate. As he became more involved in the functioning of his rural community, he watched the Western & Atlantic Railroad build its tracks across a nearby ridge that led to "Standing Peachtree," an old Cherokee trading village.

Around 1837, the rail lines joined at a point they called "Terminus." A year later, DeKalb County farmer, Meredith Collier, was elected to the state legislature. He saw the railroad junction change its name to "Marthasville" in honor of the Georgia governor's wife, Martha Lumpkin, and then in 1847, his son, John, helped draw up the charter which christened it "The

City of Atlanta." With a population of scarcely 2000 inhabitants, it was not much of a city. Rather it was a rough, frontier village with wooden buildings and muddy roads. Gradually land speculators and entrepreneurs took over to form a capitalist core and the town began to look a little more gentrified.

In 1853, Henrietta's great-grandfather, John Collier, helped draft the documents to carve Fulton County from a large portion of DeKalb; a few years later he became an original stockholder in the area's first bank. Like his father, he was active in local politics and served several terms on the city council and in the state senate. Because the Colliers owned vast portions of land, they profited from the city's growth. In 1846, John built a log cabin for his family on Nelson Street. A decade later he replaced the cabin with a large stone house fronted by a second-story verandah supported with huge columns.

John Collier was lucky during the Civil War. He was able to spirit his family out of town just before Sherman's army arrived; and when he returned, he found his Nelson Street home barely damaged. As the city rebuilt, he resumed his civic duties, an obligation soon picked up by his son Charles Augustus Collier. A lawyer like his father, he served in 1887 as leading attorney for a group of men purchasing a large tract of land on the northern outskirts of the city that would provide facilities for riding and driving horses and housing an ambitious trade show known as the Piedmont Exposition. The crowning achievement of that world's fair was the visit of President Grover Cleveland and his wife. As chairman of the Piedmont Exposition Company, Charles Collier ushered the president around town and lunched with him at the newly opened "Gentlemen's Driving Club," which occupied the old stone residence of B.F. Walker on the property.

When the fair ended, Charles Augustus Collier helped negotiate a contract in which the club sold the majority of its land to the Piedmont Exposition Company, that in turn deeded it to the city to be rechristened Piedmont Park. Eight years later, those grounds housed the well-publicized Cotton States Exposition where Tuskegee Institute president, Booker T. Washington, made his famous speech, later dubbed the "Atlanta Compromise." Collier had a major role in all events, presiding as the Exposition's president and director general, which made him one of the city's most prominent citizens. In 1897, he was elected Atlanta's mayor, a position he occupied for two one-year terms. After he left the mayor's office, the McKinley administration appointed him to be an official American Commissioner at the Paris World's Fair of 1900. During that summer, he took two trips abroad to represent his country at the international event. Three days after he returned to Atlanta from the second voyage, tragedy struck.

In the wee hours of the morning, on September 28, 1900, his family was awakened by a commotion in the backyard of their Rawson Street home. When they rushed out to see what was happening, Charles Collier lay in a pool of blood on a brick path at the foot of the porch steps. Still conscious, he said that when he heard a prowler, he grabbed his pistol and chased the intruder from the house. In the melee, his gun accidentally fired and hit him in the side. Within the hour, the former mayor's condition worsened and at 4 A.M. he died.

At that time his son, Charles Allen, was twelve years old. Within a few years he stepped into the social leadership role inherited from his ancestors. But unlike his father, grandfather, and great-grandfather, he never entered city politics. Rather he devoted his time to Atlanta commerce. Trained as an electrical engineer, he eventually became vice-president of the Georgia Power Company, a major in the Civil Air Patrol, and advisor to the Office of War Utilities during World War II. He and his wife, the former Elizabeth Sturgeon, brought up their three daughters, Elizabeth, Mary, and Henrietta, to function as Southern ladies and take part in the rituals of Atlanta society.

After graduating from the newly opened North Fulton High School, Henrietta (whose nickname was "Henny") went to Sweetbriar College in Virginia. Her roommate, Mary Elizabeth Schroder, remembers that she "had more sense" than most of the girls at Sweetbriar and was creative in everything she pursued. She was especially disposed to artistic endeavors, was a fairly accomplished amateur painter, loved surrounding herself with works of art and things of beauty, and enjoyed everything from singing and dancing to playing the piano. In keeping with the tradition that tied Atlantans to the elite of other major American cities, Henrietta Collier made her debut during the late '30s. In the social season that followed, she met Dr. William B. Armstrong, an ear-nose-throat specialist twelve years her senior and the only son of another distinguished old Atlanta family. They married in 1940, and two years later their daughter Henrietta, nicknamed "Penny," was born.

By then America was at war and Billy Armstrong was enlisted as an Army doctor, first serving in Louisiana and then following the troops overseas to North Africa and France. Shortly after her husband went to war, Henrietta gave birth to a second child, William Jr., but he lived only eighteen months and died before his father came back. Upon his return to Atlanta, Dr. Armstrong resumed his medical practice. But it didn't last long. He passed away in 1954, leaving Henrietta a young widow with a twelve-year-old daughter. "My mother did have her share of adversity" Penny observes, "and she proved herself to be a strong woman in the face of that."

Soon things began to look up. About four years before she signed up to tour Europe with the Atlanta Art Association,

Henrietta married Dr. Darrell Ayer, a brilliant pathologist who had lost his wife a few years earlier. With her adolescent daughter in tow, she moved into the West Paces Ferry Road home shared by her new husband and his two daughters. It was a happy time, Penny recalls. She found new siblings close to her own age and a new father. Her mother's artistic flair reveled in brightening up the large house which had been neglected since the first Mrs. Ayer's death.

In the fall of '61, Henrietta was organizing three debuts: that of her daughter, Penny, and step-daughters, Nancy and Jane. "I think that was somewhat of a record," Penny said. " I don't know that three daughters ever made their debuts at the same time before." During the next six months, Henrietta Ayer organized parties for each of the girls, throwing Penny's at the High Museum Coach House. The process "definitely wore Mother out ," Penny mused, and she was ready to go abroad with her friends and relax.

Lydia Black was successful in recruiting several other friends from old Atlanta families, among them Nancy and Bob Pegram. Although they had been to Europe often, they thought it would be great fun to see it again with a group of fellow Atlantans. The couple was well entrenched in old Atlanta society, although Nancy Frederick had actually been born in New York because her father was working there as an executive with the Retail Credit Corporation. While she was still a child, her family—which included her parents and older brother Claude—moved back to Atlanta and Nancy attended public school before entering Washington Seminary. A renowned beauty with auburn hair and a strikingly erect carriage, Nancy was always popular. One of her early beaux was Ivan Allen Jr., who remembered riding a bicycle to her Ansley Park home.

Her romance with Robert Baker Pegram IV began on an elevator in the Biltmore Apartments where both families lived. Although they had met occasionally at parties and their families were part of the same social group, Bob and Nancy had never paid much attention to each other. But as a result of that encounter on the elevator, they began to go out and eventually married. Born in Nashville, Tennessee, Bob Pegram—like Nancy—spent his youth away from Atlanta while his father worked as an executive for Southern Railroad. After the family came to Atlanta in the early '20s, Bob went to Boys High, then Virginia Military Institute (VMI), and received an MBA from the Harvard Business School.

By the early '40s, the Pegrams had two young daughters, Ann and Susan. Bob was employed at the First National Bank. But war was looming on the horizon, and because of his VMI education, he was in the Army Reserves. When Hitler marched through Europe, Bob became an officer in the Field Artillery, first serving in Florida and then in England and North Africa. Before the war ended, he returned to Washington to recover from a minor illness. While visiting the Pentagon to pick up his new orders, he heard a familiar voice drifting down a stairwell. Recognizing it as belonging to an old VMI buddy, he raced up the stairs only to discover that his friend had an important Pentagon job. That chance meeting landed him on the Joint Chiefs of Staff. For his service there he won the OBE, an honor that could only be granted through permission from the president.

Back in Atlanta after the war, Bob went to work for the Bank of Georgia, but soon shifted to selling life insurance, and in time retired to manage family affairs. Nancy was an active participant in volunteer work for the Junior League and remained so beautiful that her daughter, Ann Pegram Harris, remembers her mother elicited "wolf whistles" from passersby during a shopping expedition downtown. A friend also remarked about Nancy Pegram's beauty, recalling a day when they were selling tickets downtown for a musical event sponsored by the Junior League. Tired of doling out the tickets, Nancy decided to go outside and wash the window. Suddenly those inside noticed a group of men gathering on the sidewalk ogling the auburn-haired beauty. Her friends quickly suggested that she forget about the window and return to selling tickets. Bob and Nancy Pegram both took flying lessons and owned a private plane. But when they realized that solo flying was not a very sociable pursuit, they decided to direct their adventures to boating, a far more people-oriented recreation.

Their love of travel made the Art Association trip a natural and they soon persuaded their neighbors and close friends, Martha and Morris Brandon, to join them. Morris was from another prominent old Atlanta family. His paternal grandfather had come to town from a plantation in Tennessee during the 1880s, and his father was a well-respected lawyer and member of the Georgia House of Representatives. In 1947, the Atlanta Board of Education built an elementary school near Buckhead on property donated by the Brandon family and named it "Morris Brandon School" in honor of the admired lawyer. As one of three brothers, the younger Morris Brandon attended VMI with a number of Atlantans and afterwards married Martha Pritchard from Macon. When World War II began, he was shipped overseas and returned home to become a vice-president of the Bank of Georgia and owner of the Superior Syringe Company. Morris and Martha, who had no children, loved parties and were regulars at the Driving Club. When Lydia told them about the Art Association trip, it sounded like one ongoing party that they dare not miss.

Louise and Roby Robinson Jr. also wanted to join the party. They had thrown a number of their own at "Tryggvesson," later known as "the Pink Palace," a unique mansion on West Paces Ferry

Road. Louise's grandfather was Dr. Abner Wellborn Calhoun, a nationally renowned ophthalmologist, who practiced in Atlanta. His son, Andrew, and his wife, Mary Guy, built "The Pink Palace" in 1923. Designed by Neel Reid, Atlanta's best-known architect of the period, the Italianate mansion of pink and ochre stucco was modeled after baroque villas in Verona and Siena. Sunday drivers slowed down in front of its double-columned entrance to stare up at the imposing façade. But only invited guests could visit the formal gardens beneath a double-staircase in the rear of the house. Inside was a formal dining room, a drawing room, a library with paneled ceiling, five bedrooms, two sleeping porches, a sitting room, and five bathrooms—a significant luxury in 1923. When the Metropolitan Opera came to town, Enrico Caruso was said to have belted out arias at "Tryggvesson."

Roby Robinson's father had been one of the city's legendary entrepreneurs. In 1893, he established the English-American Loan & Trust Company, a small investment firm specializing in municipal bonds. A few years later, he became a director of the *Atlanta Constitution* and in 1901 joined editor, Clark Howell, to buy a controlling interest in the newspaper. Subsequently Roby Robinson Sr. became the *Constitution's* vice president and business manager. His wife, Eleanore, was one of the nine women who founded the High Museum in 1909. Meanwhile, he was expanding his investment firm by joining forces with Will Humphrey, a bond trader from Ohio. In 1902, the two men incorporated the firm of Robinson-Humphrey, which by the end of the twentieth century had become a multi-million dollar investment corporation, and a subsidiary of American Express. It joined with Solomon Smith Barney, and later became part of Citigroup.

When Roby Robinson Sr. died unexpectedly at age forty-nine in 1921, his son Roby Jr. was only thirteen. Growing up in the shadow of his illustrious parent, his namesake found himself in the center of Atlanta society. Although he began his education in the city's public schools, as a teenager he was shipped off to Switzerland to attend the Lycee-Jaccard in Laussane. Eventually he returned home and graduated from Boys High in 1925, then attended the Cheshire Academy before enrolling in Yale where he received a BA in 1931. Following his father's footsteps, he spent the next decade working at the *Atlanta Constitution* as director and advertising manager. In 1935, Roby—a stocky man known for his keen sense of humor—married Louise Phinizy Calhoun at St. Patrick's Cathedral in New York. After he returned from serving as an assistant Air Combat Intelligence officer aboard the U.S.S. *Enterprise* during World War II, he joined Robinson-Humphrey as a vice-president and director.

Also part of the old Atlanta contingent were Baxter and Julia Jones. Her grandfather, Robert J. Lowry, had been a noted banker, city councilman, and founder of the Driving Club. His Lowry National Bank handled city finances in the 1880s and '90s and he served as one of the first presidents of the Trust Company of Georgia. After several mergers during the 1920s, Lowry's bank combined with others to become Atlanta's First National Bank. Robert Lowry was best known, however, for his "tally-ho," an elaborate carriage and horses that propelled him around town. In the early twentieth century, "Colonel" Lowry could be seen sitting in his coach-and-four at the Driving Club overlooking Piedmont Park.

His daughter, Julia, married Bates Block, a distinguished doctor trained in Europe, who taught neurology at Emory Medical School. Julia was active in the Atlanta Art Association during the 1920s, an appreciation that her daughter, also named Julia, inherited. The Blocks were not only attuned to the fine arts, but aware of popular culture as well. When their daughter, Julia, "came out" in 1939, her family imported Guy Lombardo and his band to play for her debutante ball. Shortly after her debut, Julia began dating Baxter Jones, son of a prominent Macon, Georgia, attorney and her brother Bates's best friend at Emory Law School. They married around the time that Baxter enlisted as a private in the Army and the couple began their life together at a military base in Delaware. By the war's end, he had risen in the ranks to become a major. After finishing his tour of duty, he returned to Atlanta, finished at Emory, passed the Georgia bar, and joined the law firm of Sutherland, Tuttle & Brennan. During that time, Jones developed an interest in local politics, culminating in an unsuccessful campaign for Congress in 1952. A year earlier, the couple's daughter Julia arrived, followed by the birth of two sons, Baxter in 1957 and Douglas in 1960.

While caring for home and family, Julia Jones also found time to be an active volunteer. With quiet efficiency, she presided over the Atlanta Junior League, the Woman of the Year Committee, and the Opera Guild, in addition to participating in garden clubs and working for the Art Association. Her friends remember her as a gentle, reticent person, who always dressed beautifully with elegant but quiet taste. This sensitivity came through in her love of the fine arts. During her youth, Julia had taken classes at the High Museum and continued to paint as an adult. The Browne Decorating Company so admired her paintings that they bought some to be used in homes they were furnishing.

Julia infected her husband with her passion for art. Shortly before they left for Paris, they purchased a painting entitled *Adam and Eve* done by the Mexican artist, Leonardo Nierman. *Atlanta Constitution* editor, Eugene Patterson, described it: "two angular birds fly side by side—one white, one gold." He had seen the painting when he and his wife visited the Jones's Tuxedo Road home during the spring of '62. He remarked that it looked "like an airplane flying into a storm," and Jones replied, "it kind of does, doesn't it."

The Robinsons, Brandons, Pegrams, and Joneses had much in common. The men served as officers in World War II while their wives performed volunteer services for the Junior League and other charities. All had tangential or direct ties to old Atlanta families, which entitled them to belong to a privileged class. By virtue of longevity, their ancestors had provided them a niche at the pinnacle of the city's social hierarchy. From christenings to funerals, debutante balls to Junior League meetings, they traveled in close proximity.

Like Henrietta Ayer, Lydia Black, Anne Merritt, and many of the women traveling with the Art Association, they lived in the lush wooded neighborhood that radiated northwest from the Buckhead shopping area. Their city orbited around a pyramidal universe and they occupied comfortable seats at the top. Most felt certain their way of life would continue for generations. Their daughters and granddaughters would "come out" at the Driving Club, join the Junior League, and socialize only with other white Christians. Their sons and sons-in-law would run the banks and major businesses. Their city, now in the hands of a member of their group, would continue to respond to a power-structure comprised of close friends and business colleagues. But as Martin Luther King Jr. spoke at rallies and African American ladies made their first timid attempts to try-on dresses at Rich's, the foundations of Atlanta society were cracking.

CHAPTER 4

❧ From Commerce to Community

*I*n December 1960, slightly over a year before he became mayor, Ivan Allen Jr. was inaugurated as president of the Atlanta Chamber of Commerce. One of his main projects was pushing the city's second "Forward Atlanta" campaign, the first having taken place in the late 1920s under the leadership of his father, also a Chamber president. The purpose of both endeavors was to entice business and industry to relocate in the metropolitan area. Because Atlanta's employment rate lagged behind its population, the Chamber aspired to generate more new business in hopes of promoting the Georgia capital as a national commercial hub.

Growth had been Atlanta's byword since its founding, and when Allen entered the mayor's office in January 1962, the city was on a springboard poised to leap. For several years, a lighted sign on Peachtree Road had been flashing the mounting population tally. Although the exact count was impossible to calculate, the Chamber of Commerce figured that metropolitan residents topped the million mark in October 1959, which made it the largest city in the Southeast, ranking twenty-second in the nation. No one suggested that the growth should slow down. Instead the Chamber proudly sought to induce more people to move to the metropolitan area.

A recent Agnes Scott graduate named Susan Coltrane was one of those enthusiastic about Atlanta. Her boss, George Goodwin, ran the marketing department of the First National Bank (now Wachovia), which included "Commercial Business Planning," a polite cover for public relations and the bank's corporate-citizen role. Goodwin—who began his career as a newspaper reporter—realized that in order to persuade people to relocate a business or industry in Atlanta, the city had to present itself as a Mecca of urbane sophistication. In the early '60s, Goodwin was well aware that his hometown was not only sadly behind in its cultural offerings but its sports agenda also fell far short of its northern counterparts. Working with the city power structure and the Chamber of Commerce, Goodwin and Coltrane began to create images of a stable city run by a coterie of responsible bankers and other commercial giants dedicated to maintaining racial harmony, promoting the arts, and improving leisure time activities.

One of the businessmen involved in the "Forward Atlanta" campaign was Del Paige, who headed both the Arts Association board and the Cultural Needs Committee, then hoping to gain the city's cooperation in funding a performing arts center. In addition, Paige ran the Atlanta branch of Ernst & Ernst, one of the top eight nationwide accounting firms. His office was in the same First National Bank Building where George Goodwin and Susan Coltrane were publicizing the city. Perhaps at his bidding—

or more likely as an evolutionary process—an idea hatched. The Art Association's European tour might actually aid the "Forward Atlanta" campaign. If the city's leaders were traveling abroad to study the arts, then they would project the image that Atlanta was a cultured community filled with art lovers. In other words, participants were not tourists; they were cultural emissaries.

It was partly for this reason that Susan Coltrane decided to sign up for the trip. She had been planning to go to Europe anyway that spring with her friend, Jean Higgins, thinking that a journey abroad might provide the perfect respite for broadening her horizons. With this in mind, she resigned from her job at the bank, obtained a passport, and made reservations. But a week before their scheduled departure, Jean's father died unexpectedly and she could not leave her mother alone. Susan had her suitcase packed and no place to go. In those days, a single woman in her mid-twenties rarely traveled alone, and certainly not in uncharted territory.

Then the solution presented itself. Lydia Black—a family friend, who also worshipped at the First Presbyterian Church—told her that there were still a few remaining seats on the Air France charter. Thus shortly before the May 9 departure, Susan Coltrane cast her lot with the Art Association in order to take her long-anticipated trip to Europe.

Margaret Turner was a link between the Forward Atlanta boosters and the Art Association tour. As club editor and feature writer for the *Atlanta Journal,* she had arranged to travel as a press representative and record the journey for the paper. A native Atlantan, Turner began her career in journalism during World War II, when she worked for the Atlanta Chapter of the American Red Cross as a volunteer staff assistant with the task of editing their monthly magazine. When the war ended, she joined the staff of the *Atlanta Journal*. Her columns covered what was considered to be "women's stuff," which in the 1950s and early '60s meant art exhibitions, auctions, shopping news, and home decorating. Fellow columnist, Doris Lockerman, commented that Turner was "a very effective reporter," but in the newspaper world she never received "quite the prestige she would have gotten if she had been writing about business subjects." Nevertheless, Margaret Turner commanded the respect of her colleagues because of her perceptive reporting in a clear, readable style. Her husband Paul had died in 1961, and everyone agreed that the trip would be good for her. She had never been to Europe and combining work with pleasure was a temptation she could not resist.

One of her traveling companions was Rosalind Janes Williams, an advertising executive with strong ties to Atlanta journalism. Divorced in 1956 and inching closer to retirement, the chance to tour abroad came along at the perfect time. Few women were considered business professionals in 1962, but Williams was an exception. Not only was she tops in her field and recipient of numerous awards for her outstanding work, but she had an uncanny capacity to meet and understand people. A native of Griffin, Georgia, Rosalind graduated from Agnes Scott College in 1925 and stayed in Atlanta to take a job as a fashion writer for Rich's. Within a few years, she achieved notice for her original ideas and brilliant flair for department store advertising. In 1930, she married Charlie Williams, a former University of Georgia football star with a degree from the Chicago Art Institute. They built a house on Club Drive, north of Buckhead, where they raised their two children, Linda and Bill.

All the while, Rosalind was a working mother. After leaving Rich's she took a job with the advertising department at Davison-Paxon, the Macy's affiliate, later known simply as

Davison's. Gradually this petite and talented woman worked her way up to be the store's advertising manager, a job she retained for more than sixteen years. Recognized in her profession for her uncanny ability to push the right buttons with her clever and informative copy, she added a personal touch to otherwise routine advertising. For a few years Rosalind Williams channeled this skill into a weekly newspaper column entitled "Today on Peachtree," which ran alongside Davison's full-page ad. More than just promotional jargon, her column combined subtle public relations with human interest stories.

For three consecutive years during the early '50s, her ads for Davison's won distinctive merit awards from the National Retail Dry Goods Association, and in 1955 she was named Atlanta's Woman of the Year in the professions. Two years later, the journalism society, Theta Sigma Phi, gave her their "Brenda" citation for outstanding advertising. After a long career at Davison's, Rosalind left the store to become vice president of Tucker-Wayne, one of Atlanta's largest advertising agencies. Despite her active career, she found time to work for a number of charities, her favorite being the Atlanta Fashion Group, an informal gathering of women involved in fashion-oriented journalism. Rosalind—who once won "Atlanta's Best Dressed in Business" award—was one of the most stylish members of the group in her unusual hats and chic business outfits.

Rosalind Williams was not the only person in the advertising and publishing industry to sign up for the Art Association trip. Also traveling with the group was her co-worker at Tucker-Wayne, Lysle Williamson, the recently elected president of the Atlanta chapter of American Women in Radio and Television; and Henry Redfern (Red) Hollins, director of Research and Promotion for W.R.C. Smith Publishing Company. An Englishman by birth, Red Hollins, traveling with his wife Celia, was one of the creators of the new "Forward Atlanta" campaign. As a personable and generous leader in the community, Red chaired the Chamber of Commerce's committee that began publishing *Atlanta Magazine* in 1961. Traveling with the Hollins's was the board chairman of W.R.C. Smith, William J. Rooke, and his wife Birtie.

Tom Chris Allen was also part of the advertising and publishing contingent. Born in Durant, Oklahoma in 1907, he attended the University of Oklahoma where he discovered his talents as a writer and met Dorothy (Pat) Mills, daughter of a Tulsa physician. After his graduation, they married and Tom Chris Allen embarked on a career in journalism. This large man in stature and congeniality was a whiz at producing advertising copy. In 1937, he joined the staff of *Life* and subsequently became the magazine's Southeastern Advertising Manager. That meant he, Pat, and their two sons—Tom Chris Jr. (or T.C.) and Ben—had to relocate in Atlanta. With Tom Chris's outgoing joviality and Pat's warm friendliness, the Allen's entertained frequently in their gracious home on Tuxedo Road. Neither of them had ever been to Europe, although it had been a long-time dream for the Oklahoma couple and they were excited about going.

Many of these advertising and publishing executives were active members of the Chamber of Commerce and they could justify taking time off from work because they considered themselves to be cultural emissaries. As astute participants in the latest "Forward Atlanta" campaign, they could rationalize three weeks of fun as helping Atlanta publicize its image and increase its commercial potential.

With its veneer of modern buildings, Atlanta appeared to be the antithesis of a Southern city. Yet despite the recently exploding civil rights movement unfolding in its midst, the city still clung to old patterns of segregation. Sometimes it took newcomers to facilitate Jim Crow's exit. One was Saul Gerson, a native of Odessa, Russia. He came to the United States when he was a small child and worked his way up in the tough New York business world until he was able to open a hat factory in Greenwich Village. By then he had married Mildred Wasserman—who was born in Boston but grew up in New York—and had two children, Robert (Bob) and Betsy. His hat business floundered during the Depression and by 1940 Gerson had to declare bankruptcy and close the factory. For the previous few years, Mildred had suffered from chronic bronchitis and was advised by her doctors to move out of New York. Saul had been to Atlanta and liked it, so shortly after his business failed he relocated his family.

Upon arrival in the Georgia capital, Gerson got a job running a hat factory on Prior Street and eventually became general manager for a hat manufacturing plant in Red Oak, Georgia. Within a few years, he was able to pay back all of his New York creditors, a generous and rare gesture that encouraged many of his sources and vendors to assist him in founding a new business. In 1945, he opened a men's custom hatter in downtown Atlanta called Robley Hats, a conflation of his son's name and that of a neighbor's son, Stanley. Soon the business caught on and at last Saul Gerson was a success.

When Bob came to work with his father in 1959, an African American employee named Robert Campbell made hats at the rear of the store. Customers would walk in the front door and go directly back to have Campbell adjust or shape their hats. Since he was so popular, Saul decided to make him a salesman, but following Southern customs, he made sure that either he or Bob rang up the sale. One day Bob suggested that as long as Campbell was selling the hats, he might as well operate the cash register, an unprecedented occurrence in still-segregated Atlanta. That made Robley Hats one of the first businesses in Atlanta to have an integrated staff.

An entire generation of Atlanta businessmen were being gradually reeducated. Even those with roots in the rural South were having to face inevitable change. Sykes Young, one of the city's leading accountants, embraced new ideas with an open mind. His ascent from farm boy to executive typified the entrepreneurial spirit that fueled Atlanta's growth. His future wife, Carroll MacDonald, lived comfortably in Fitzgerald, a south Georgia town established during the 1890s as a planned community to honor both Union and Confederate soldiers. Her father, the son of a Scottish immigrant, made a fortune in land speculation and was an officer of the local bank. But he died when Carroll was seven and his business partners slowly drove his estate into the ground. Although her two older sisters attended Agnes Scott, Carroll could go no further than high school because the now-depleted bank account had nothing left for college tuition.

While Carroll had a taste of the good life before the money vanished, Sykes Young grew up in a household of hardworking farmers in Irwin County, a few miles south of Fitzgerald, and spent his youth making cane syrup and killing hogs. Because education was always important in his family he walked a mile down the dirt road to a one-room schoolhouse. Always an industrious pupil who excelled in math, Sykes applied for a scholarship to the U.S. Military Academy at West Point. He qualified for admission, but only one applicant from Georgia could receive the appointment and he was second in line.

After that disappointment, Sykes left home at age sixteen and worked in south Georgia for awhile before coming back to Fitzgerald and auditing books for local companies. But when he married Carroll MacDonald in 1930, he realized he would have to advance his career in order to support her in the lifestyle she had lost but hoped to regain. Consequently he studied to become a Certified Public Accountant and in this capacity took his new wife and her mother to Rome, Georgia, where he became the city's accountant. That job ended when he discovered fraud in the municipal bookkeeping and exposed it to the community. Finding life in Rome too difficult after challenging local authorities, the Youngs and Mrs. MacDonald moved to Atlanta and settled in a Decatur apartment where they lived when their only child, Carroll, was born in 1934.

Shortly after his arrival in Atlanta, Sykes Young teamed up with another accountant named Al Garber to form the firm of Young & Garber. Because Al Garber was Jewish, this was the beginning of Young's experience in understanding and befriending people of different backgrounds. Their close partnership proved to be an unbeatable combination, attracting both Jewish and Christian clients, and they handled the taxes for most of Atlanta's prominent families, including many of those who signed up for the Art Association trip. While working with Garber, Young was also advancing his education. With the goal of becoming both an accountant and tax lawyer, he acquired an undergraduate business degree from night school and a Bachelors of Law and Masters of Law in Federal Taxation.

Always the entrepreneur, Young built an interest in and served as president of the Marble Products Company, which operated a quarry in north Georgia, and he also owned stock and served on the boards of a number of other local corporations. Young's growing fortunes facilitated his family's ascent up the social ladder. They bought a large home off of West Paces Ferry Road where he and Carroll shared a love of gardening that turned their home into a showplace. He joined the Capital City Club, took up golf, and participated in a weekly card game at the club, while Carroll, who loved to meet people, became a volunteer at Piedmont Hospital and a docent at a few historical houses. Their daughter attended Washington Seminary and then Vanderbilt

University, where she met and married Allen Cargile, whose family was prominent in Nashville society. In short, they had succeeded both financially and socially.

Now it was time for them to venture abroad. At the bidding of their close friends Tommy and Nell Lanier, the Youngs signed up for the Art Association flight. They would take the chartered plane and travel with the Laniers following a more-or-less parallel course with the escorted tour before spending a few days with Nell Lanier's brother, William R. Hunnicutt, the captain of a destroyer stationed in the Mediterranean.

The Youngs and Laniers had much in common. Nell loved to garden and to meet people while Tommy, like Sykes, was a workaholic and had come to Atlanta for business reasons. Born in Winchester, Tennessee, in 1912, Tommy was the youngest of John Hicks Lanier's four children. The family moved to Nashville while he was young and Thomas Lanier followed his older brother Sartain (Sot) to Vanderbilt University. After graduation in 1934, he joined his two brothers at the Lanier Company, a distributor for Edison dictating machines in the Southeast. In the late '30s, they moved the business headquarters to Atlanta. Because Tommy's territory was North and South Carolina, he decided to live in that area to be nearer to his customers.

On a trip to Atlanta to visit his brothers and attend a Georgia Tech football game, he met Nell Hunnicutt, a sophomore at Oglethorpe University. Her family was from the Atlanta area, although they then lived on a farm in Norcross a few miles north of town. Nell spent much of her youth in Tampa, Florida, where her father, Reese Hunnicutt, had moved during the '20s in hopes of making a fortune in the land boom. By the time she graduated from Plant High School in Tampa, the boom turned to bust and her family headed back to Atlanta. Bill Hunnicutt had begun college at the University of Florida but transferred when he received an appointment to the Naval Academy at Annapolis.

Nell and Tommy married in 1937 and settled first in Greensboro, North Carolina, and then in Charlotte. While he traveled around selling dictating machines, Nell attended Queens College in Charlotte until her daughter Linda was born in 1941. The next year they moved to Atlanta. By then, the United States had entered World War II, and the Laniers jumped on the bandwagon by buying a pants factory in north Georgia to make trousers for the armed services. That required splitting their operation in half. The eldest brother, Hicks, ran the dictating machine section, while Tommy and "Sot" took over the new apparel business, known as Oxford Manufacturing Company. After the war, Oxford expanded by opening sewing plants throughout the Southeast to produce a variety of clothing for both men and women. Sartain Lanier was the chief financial officer while Tommy ran the plants and supervised the employees.

After coming to Atlanta, Tommy and Nell had two more children, Reese (born in 1943) and Nancy (born in 1947); and they eventually moved into a rambling house on a five-acre lot. To expedite visiting the sewing plants around the South, the company bought two airplanes and Nell and Tommy—along with Sartain and his wife, Claudia—became licensed pilots. The double purchase was to insure that Oxford would never lose both chief executives. For further safety, Sot always flew with Nell, and Tommy traveled with Claudia. If one of the planes went down, their children would still have one parent left.

By 1962, as they prepared to go to Europe together, Tommy and Nell Lanier were not worried about flying together. The children were older now and pretty self-sufficient. Linda had just finished her junior year at Goucher and was planning to be married in a small wedding at the National Cathedral in Washington a week after her parents' return. Reese was finally graduating from high school, having played his way through two private schools before landing at Northside, a large public school near their home. There was much going on, but the Laniers hated to turn down the chance to travel on this very inviting three-week odyssey.

Vasser Woolley Jr. was also trying to escape. Although his wife had been dead for more than a year, he was still in mourning. It was a good time to take advantage of the cheap Air France charter fare and visit his sister, Mildred, who had a home in Belgium. Before the term "people person" was part of the American vernacular, Vasser Woolley fit the description. With his relaxed and outgoing personality and penchant for entertaining, Vasser was one of Atlanta's most compelling characters and most successful businessmen. Born in Atlanta in 1897, he and his older sister, Mildred, grew up in a house built by their father on the corner of Spring and Twelfth Streets. During World War I, Vasser left Georgia Tech to join the Army, but he somehow negotiated to receive a chemical engineering degree from Tech without ever officially graduating. After returning from overseas, he went to work for the laboratory in New Jersey owned by Thomas Edison.

Meanwhile, Mildred married Belgian chemist Paul Seydel, who ran dye-making plants in New Jersey and West Virginia. An economic recession in 1923 forced him to relocate in Atlanta where Georgia's expanding textile market seemed the perfect location to manufacture industrial dyes. When his first partner left suddenly, Paul asked Vasser to come into the business, which became known as Seydel-Woolley & Company.

While they were living in West Virginia, Mildred had begun working as a columnist for the Charleston Gazette, adding another "l" to her last name to create the pen name "Mildred Seydell." Upon her return home, she joined the staff of the *Atlantan Georgian,* owned by William Randolph Hearst, working her way up to a syndicated column that allowed her to travel around the world interviewing celebrities.

When Mildred's father died in 1928, Paul Seydel moved his wife and two sons (Paul Jr. and John) into the Spring Street house, and Vasser occupied an apartment in the basement. Then in the late '30s, he moved into a log cabin nearby at 1078 Williams Street. Originally built for a "party house," this house was gradually transformed into a permanent residence. The outside may have looked rugged, but the inside was innovative and luxurious; he even preserved a tree that grew through the center of the living room. Nothing was conventional, especially the owner.

With the onset of another World War, Vasser again donned a uniform, this time as a member of the Civil Air Patrol. Now considered one of the city's most eligible bachelors, the balding bon vivant entertained lavishly in his log cabin lodged in the shadow of downtown. Then in 1942, his brother-in-law died and Vasser became chairman of the chemical company. A few years later, Mildred married Paul's brother, Max, and moved with him to Belgium, although she still retained the family home in Atlanta. Suddenly in the late '40s, Vasser surprised everyone by marrying his secretary, Audrey Pate.

Around that time, the Department of Transportation was preparing to build the city's first expressway through the middle of Vasser's property. Refusing to abandon his house, he simply moved it a few blocks away to Techwood Drive, near the Georgia Tech campus. He could not move the tree growing through the living room, so he replaced it in the new location with a glassed-in waterfall that contained an old waterwheel generated by electricity.

Audrey died of cancer in 1961, and even though he had been a bachelor for so many years, Vasser suffered greatly. The parties he once loved lost their luster, and he spent most of his time looking after his aging mother. In early '62, Mildred found out about the Air France charter to Paris and convinced her brother to visit her in Belgium.

Dr. Harry Boon came to Atlanta from his hometown of Wilmington, North Carolina after working as a lifeguard and railroad worker in order to earn his tuition to the Atlanta Dental College (later part of Emory University). After receiving his degree in the early '20s, he went into practice in downtown Atlanta. Around that time, he had a blind date with an Agnes Scott Latin major from Newnan, named Mary Mann. Two years after her graduation in 1924, they married and eventually purchased a house on Bolling Road where they brought up their two children, Ann and Harry Jr.

By then Dr. Boon had transferred his practice into the W.W. Orr Doctor's Building, a modern facility in a converted apartment building on Peachtree. A perfectionist in his profession, he also loved to have fun. In between appointments, Harry would retreat to the doctor's lounge in the basement to smoke cigars and play cards. As an avid, if playful, fisherman, he once pulled an abscessed tooth out of the mouth of a captured fish; and during World War II, he left a string of fish on the pier so that navy fighter planes could use it for target practice. Having diverse interests and orientation, Harry was also a licensed pilot, a mandolin player, a Shriner, and a participating member of the Capital City and Piedmont Driving Clubs. Mary Boon was equally as independent and varied in her interests, which ranged from book clubs to weight lifting. In 1962, she began taking painting lessons at the Art Association and found out about the European tour. Since her graduation from Agnes Scott, she had wanted to travel abroad and the Art Association tour provided a perfect way to fulfill that dream.

Allen Pierce McDonald, traveling with his wife Adelaide, was the other dentist on the trip. Born into a Bolton, Georgia, medical family, Pierce received his undergraduate and dental degrees from Emory before becoming a Navy Lieutenant in the

Dental Corps during World War II. Adelaide, a native of Black Mountain, North Carolina, graduated from the Women's College of the University of North Carolina. At the time of their departure for Europe, their three sons ranged in age from eleven to twenty-three. The MacDonalds had taken an interest in the Atlanta Arts Association, perhaps because Adelaide's sister, Eleanor Storza, was such an active member.

Many of the people planning to take the trip were patients of Dr. Christopher McLoughlin, a diagnostician on the staff of Piedmont Hospital specializing in diabetes and arthritis. His practice with Drs. William Minnich and Lewis Paullin administered to the city's upper crust. A native of Philadelphia, McLoughlin came to Atlanta as a soldier during World War II and decided to stay. Perhaps one of the reasons was Jane Sharp, whose family was quite prominent in the city. Her father had worked his way up from being a pots-and-pans salesman to operating a successful hardware wholesale business. By the time their two children, Jack and Jane, came along the Sharps were members of the Piedmont Driving Club, where Jane made her debut in 1931.

She attended Oglethorpe University and Johns Hopkins before marrying Chris McLoughlin in 1942. Several years later, they bought a house on Hillside Drive, north of Buckhead, large enough to house both of Jane's parents and their two sons, Chris Jr. and Norman. While Dr. McLoughlin practiced at Piedmont Hospital, he participated in numerous professional societies with a special interest in the American Diabetes Association. Jane joined the Cherokee chapter of the DAR and became chairman of the Fifth District Woman's Auxiliary of the Fulton County Medical Association. They had been to Europe several times, but this trip intrigued them both. Jane could travel for awhile with her friends and then go with Chris to a medical convention in Italy.

The legal profession was also well represented on the Art

Association tour by Baxter Jones, Morgan Cantey, Sykes Young, Arnold Kaye, and Reuben Crimm. Both Kaye and Crimm came from Jewish families, although by 1962, Kaye had no formal religious affiliation. The Brooklyn-born lawyer attended NYU where he adapted a liberal mindset that labeled him a radical when he came to Atlanta with his parents and younger brother during the 1930s. Nevertheless, he stuck to his controversial opinions at Atlanta Law School and during his early years as a fledgling attorney at the firm headed by Herbert Haas. It was during those early years of practice that he met Gladys Jones.

Their romance played like a scene from *Guys and Dolls*. Gladys had been born in Tunica, Mississippi, but the family settled in Vicksburg in time for her to enter elementary school. She was a star student and model child, always held up as an example for her eight younger siblings. In Depression-ridden Mississippi there were few opportunities for a bright young girl, so when family friends and officers in the Salvation Army suggested that Gladys move with them to their new commission in Tuscaloosa, Alabama, she readily complied. After graduating from high school there, she enrolled in the Salvation Army's officer's training program. By then she had become a beauty, with long black hair, gentle blue eyes, and an endearing warm smile. When a work assignment in downtown Atlanta brought the eighteen-year-old Salvation Army trainee to the attention of Arnold Kaye, it was love at first sight.

After what must have been an intriguing courtship, they married in 1940. A year later, with the country at war, Arnold entered the Army's Officers' Candidate School in Moses Lake, Washington. Gladys followed him there and to Washington, D.C., where he was assigned to the Army's legal branch. At war's end, they returned to Atlanta and Arnold went back to the same law firm. Soon after their return, their first son Arnold Jr., whom they called "Beau," was born and his brother Richard (Rick) arrived a few years later. They built a home on Douglas Road near Sandy Springs, filled their large lot with a variety of pets and wildlife, and the boys kept a horse at a nearby stable. As the children became self-sufficient, Gladys returned to service work, devoting many volunteer hours to Grady Hospital's children's ward and the Big Sister's organization for underprivileged girls.

Arnold was an avid collector with a particular affinity for traditional paintings and antiques, some of which he donated to the High Museum. His interests were quite eclectic. For relaxation, he often played pinochle or strummed his banjo in an informal musical group with a violinist from the Atlanta Symphony and his brother-in-law, Jake Goldstein, who played both piano and trombone. Despite the Kayes' cultural interests, they had never been to Europe, so when the Art Association trip came up, it seemed like the perfect time for them to view the great masters at first hand and add some to their own collection.

Reuben Crimm, another lawyer on the trip, was a native Atlantan. His father, Isadore, had been an itinerant optometrist, traveling through South Carolina and Alabama checking eyes and selling glasses. Reuben worked his way through the University of Georgia, Atlanta Branch (now Georgia State University) and received a degree from the Woodrow Wilson Law School before moving to Washington to clerk in the Judge Adjutant General's office. While serving in this position during World War II, he met Janet (Jan) Fishman, the youngest of four daughters of an Oklahoma City physician. She had left the University of Michigan to work for the "war effort" by volunteering for government agencies in the nation's capital.

After the war, they settled in Atlanta, where their three children, Allan, Nina, and Walter (now Walt) were born. Reuben developed a successful practice as a transportation attorney, handling cases all over the country, while Jan did a great deal of volunteer work for the League of Women Voters and Council of Jewish Women. They built a home on Old Ivy Road and became active members of the community. Because of Reuben's profession, he traveled constantly and often took Jan with him. But they always managed to find time for family vacations, usually annual trips to the beach. Reuben and Jan had been to Europe before and to Mexico. When they received the Art Association brochure, they decided to take the Air France charter so they could travel to Egypt, Israel, Turkey, and Greece with their good friends, Florette and Louis Patz from Elberton, Georgia.

This diverse assortment of executives and professionals composed a distinctive coterie to represent their city in Europe. Not all of them were following the escorted tour, but those who were went with an understanding that they would be spreading the word about Atlanta. As representatives of the business, legal, and medical communities, they were determined to demonstrate that Atlantans could be more cultured and worldly than other Americans, and perhaps even match Europeans in their urbane sophistication.

CHAPTER 5

❧ *Atlanta vs. Georgia*

A decade before C. Baxter Jones Jr. embarked on the Atlanta Art Association trip to Europe, he challenged his state's political establishment, a formidable task he had been pursuing for several years. After his discharge from the Army in 1946, Jones became active in Georgia's political affairs. In 1950, when at age thirty-one he was selected by the Atlanta Junior Chamber of Commerce as "The Man of the Year," he stated that his goal was to improve state government. That was a daunting ambition, because at that time, state politics were dominated by rural Democrats, who supported the national party but ranted against the liberal Yankees dominating it.

That hatred was enhanced by Atlanta's *bête noir*, the county-unit system, a convoluted regulation that was Georgia's unbalanced equivalent to the electoral college. In the Democratic primaries that virtually determined the outcome of every state election, the rule assigned "units" to each of the 159 counties—the most in any of the states—based on geographical boundaries. Small rural counties had two units, the larger urban ones six. But as the population shifted to the metropolitan centers during the early twentieth century, the law remained unchanged. This meant that the rapidly growing cities, especially Atlanta, were underrepresented while the smaller farming counties with shrinking populations wielded disproportionate power.

In the same year that Baxter Jones was named JC "Man of the Year," a formidable team of Atlanta attorneys, led by Morris Abram and Hamilton Douglas Jr., challenged the county-unit system in federal court. But the effort failed when the local panel of judges ruled that a state's voting laws were not a federal matter, a decision upheld by the U.S. Supreme Court. When Governor Herman Talmadge tried to amend the state constitution to make the county-unit system mandatory in all elections, Baxter Jones formed and chaired a state-wide, non-partisan citizens' group to oppose the amendment. His efforts convinced the public to vote by a 30,000 margin against the county-unit system. But it was a hollow victory with no real means of implementation.

Preservation or destruction of the county-unit system was the central issue in the 1952 Democratic Primary for Atlanta's Congressional seat. The two leading contestants were the incumbent, James C. Davis, and his principal opponent, C. Baxter Jones Jr. Georgia's Fifth Congressional District was then composed of three counties: Fulton, DeKalb, and Rockdale. Fulton was predominantly urban, but most of DeKalb and all of Rockdale were conservative and largely rural, so their combined eight units outweighed more heavily populated Fulton's six. Although Davis lost the popular vote in the election of 1946, the right-wing DeKalb judge won the election because of the county-unit system. Baxter Jones was quite popular with Atlanta voters and had many influential contacts. Throughout the 1952 campaign, he promised that if elected he would end the county-unit system and hinted that he wanted to eliminate the disastrous conditions of the state's segregated Negro schools.

The Davis backers of DeKalb County countered with an ad revealing that Jones taught courses at Atlanta University and Morehouse College. "The philosophy of a man who teaches before and among members of the colored race," the ad stated, "cannot possibly" avoid the influence of blacks and would bring about the "end of segregation of the races and of many other long seated traditions of the South." A vote for Jones, the Davis backers insisted, was a vote for "the radical left-wing Eastern press."

With a strong backing from the black community and the Atlanta business establishment, Jones won the popular vote in the Democratic primary of 1952. But the county-unit votes of Rockdale and DeKalb Counties combined to give Davis the nomination, a victory that kept him in Congress for another decade. And it would take just that long for the county-unit system to receive a challenge as strong as that leveled by C. Baxter Jones Jr. His partner, Elbert Tuttle, consoled Jones by insisting that he had the best of both worlds, because he won the election but did not have to serve.

Morgan Cantey and Baxter Jones had a great deal in common. Both were born in small Georgia towns and both graduated from Emory Law School, although Cantey finished there five years earlier than Jones. His family was typical of so many small-town Southerners in the early twentieth century. Both parents were natives of South Carolina, who settled in Ashburn, Georgia, where Morgan Sabb Cantey Sr. operated the local dry goods store. His son and namesake was born in that quiet community in 1911, attended local public schools, and entered Emory as an undergraduate when he was only sixteen.

When Cantey first arrived, the suburban Atlanta campus was relatively new. Founded originally in 1836 as a small Methodist college in Oxford, Georgia, Emory received a million-dollar grant from Coca-Cola founder, Asa G. Candler to build a campus on a seventy-five-acre wooded lot in Druid Hills. In 1916, the law and theology buildings were completed and three years later the undergraduate facilities opened, only nine years before Morgan Cantey entered as a freshman. The tall, intense brunette was a serious student, but left time for playing basketball, participating in intercollegiate debating, and joining the Chi Phi fraternity. Immediately after receiving his bachelor's degree, Morgan Cantey entered Emory Law School and received his degree in 1934. For a few years he practiced in Atlanta, but aware that the United States would probably enter the war, he signed up for Officer Candidate School in early 1941.

At that time, he was courting a young teacher named Elizabeth Acree, an intelligent young woman with dark, sympathetic eyes. Upon hearing that the Japanese had bombed Pearl Harbor, Morgan proposed. The young couple had similar backgrounds. She had grown up in the small Georgia town of Greenville and attended Wesleyan, a Methodist college in Macon. Everyone called her "Ted," a nickname she acquired in elementary school. When they married in February 1942, her father—then pastor of the First Methodist Church in Rome Georgia—performed the ceremony. After the wedding, Ensign Cantey served as a naval intelligence officer, completing his tour of duty as a Lieutenant Commander in charge of amphibious forces in the Pacific.

After the war, Morgan and Ted settled in West Point, Georgia, near the Alabama border where her parents then lived. Their daughter Ann was born in 1943, and three years later, her sister Beth came along, followed in 1951 by Morgan Jr. For several years, Cantey practiced law in West Point and in 1954 became chief secretary and legal counsel for the textile manufacturer West Point-Pepperell, the top industry in the area. The Canteys were thus considered leading citizens of the community and their home was always filled with local and international guests. Ted was such a consummate hostess that she once drank the contents of her own finger bowl to keep a foreign visitor from realizing that he had committed a *faux pas.*

In addition to his family and his work, Morgan Cantey had two passionate interests: Emory University and the Methodist Church. Always actively involved with his alma mater, he was elected as an Alumni Trustee in 1955, a post he held with great enthusiasm for two terms. During those years, he also served as a steward of the First Methodist Church of West Point; he and Ted were both certified lay speakers of the North Georgia Methodist Conference and traveled across the state delivering lectures.

Through their close friends the Henry Bowdens and other Emory colleagues, the Canteys learned of the Atlanta Art Association tour and decided to go. Their daughter Ann was then a freshman at Randolph-Macon Women's College in Virginia, and her father was busy writing her every day. She would be home shortly before they left and had agreed to watch over sixteen-year-old Beth and ten-year-old Morgan Jr. while their parents were away. The low price of the Air France ticket was too tempting to refuse. They would fly to Paris with the group and tour Italy and Spain on their own.

On the other side of the state in the small town of Elberton, another couple was arranging for care of their three children while they toured Europe. They shared with the Canteys the easy-going lifestyle of a warm, Southern community. But otherwise their backgrounds were entirely different. Louis and Florette Patz were both Jewish and that distinguished them from the predominantly Protestant population of their small Southern town. Louis Patz lived all of his life in Elberton, located 100 miles east of Atlanta. The story of his ancestors' sojourn from eastern Europe to eastern Georgia is a tale of strong ethnic pride and grateful assimilation.

Louis's grandfather, Max Berman, came to America in 1882 from Kovno, Lithuania. At age twenty-nine, he left his pregnant wife, Rachel, and two children in search of a better life across the Atlantic. Traveling with a few friends, he landed in Baltimore and headed south peddling goods with a horse and wagon. In 1889, seven years after reaching the United States, he opened a small general store in a suburb of Charleston, South Carolina and accumulated enough money to send for his wife, her mother, and three children. Max had never seen his youngest child, Sarah, who was born after he departed. She was six-years-old when they reached the United States. They soon moved to Elloree, South Carolina, then to Crawfordville, Georgia, and Rachel kept having babies. To support the growing family, Max operated a small store while continuing to peddle goods in rural areas.

The family rapidly assimilated to life in the South, but Crawfordsville provided few monetary rewards, so the family moved once again. This time to Elberton, then a community of 5,000 inhabitants. Boasting of being "The Granite Capital of the World," the town's chief industry was supplying tombstones to the eastern United States. Within a few years after settling in Elberton, Max opened yet another general store and Rachel gave birth to two more children, bringing the total to nine, one of whom had died in Crawfordville. In 1903, Sarah married a young salesman named Sam Patz, who traveled around the south selling goods for the Baltimore Bargain House. For a few years, the newlyweds lived in Frogmore on the island of St. Helena off the coast of South Carolina, but when their second child arrived in 1909, they returned to Elberton, where the family helped him establish his own dry goods business. Louis, born in 1911, was the third of Sarah and Sam's six children. Max Berman had died shortly after Sarah's marriage, but Rachel Berman, continued to operate their store and was soon able to purchase a two-story brick house, a significant accomplishment for an immigrant emerging from decades of poverty.

While still running his own general store, Sam Patz became a partner in one of the town's granite companies. As virtually the only Jews in Elberton, the Bermans and Patzs were accepted by everyone, socializing with their neighbors, their children even occasionally going along with friends to the Baptist Young Peoples' Union. Sarah Patz was active in many local organizations and was chosen to be president of the Elbert County Garden Club. Often they invited Christian neighbors to their weekly Sabbath dinners, a favorite guest being the Methodist minister and his family.

By the mid-1920s, Elberton was suffering from an economic recession brought on by a boll weevil blight that had its ripple effect on the Berman and Patz stores. But the Depression of the '30s did little damage to the "Granite Capital" because people still died and still required tombstones. Therefore, Sam and Sarah remained prosperous and were able to send their son, Louis, to Cornell University to study civil engineering. But when his father had a heart attack during his sophomore year, Louis returned home to help run the store. Sam eventually recovered and was able to resume his duties, leaving Louis with little to occupy his time. So he took a part time job with Harper's Trucking Company, a firm that hauled granite from the quarries to all parts of the nation. It bothered him that the trucks left Elberton loaded with tombstones but made the return trip empty. Therefore he figured out a way to fill the returning trucks with merchandise to sell in Elberton and gradually developed Harper's into a lucrative enterprise, which he eventually took over.

Through members of their family living in Florida, Louis met Florette Cohen from New York. They married in the late forties and lived comfortably as leading citizens of the Elberton community. There they raised their three children, Sam, Harry, and Sarah Anne. While the children were encouraged to mingle freely with the Christian community, Louis and Florette maintained their Jewish traditions and attended synagogue thirty-five miles away in Athens, Georgia. Because Atlanta attorney Reuben Crimm specialized in transportation law, he represented Louis's business and over the years the two couples developed a special friendship. So when they heard about the Art Association chartered flight, they planned to fly over with the group and travel together to Greece and the Middle East.

In Marshallville, a tiny town in the middle of Georgia near Macon, Louise and Robert (Bob) Turner were making similar plans. Like the Canteys in West Point and the Patzs in Elberton, the Turners were pillars of the small community. Born in 1910 in nearby Hawkinsville, Bob Turner was a banker and gentleman farmer. Louise's family had been in Marshallville since the 1850s. Her father managed a large farm and also ran the only merchandise establishment in the rural town.

When Louise Taylor was nine years old, she wrote in her diary that she wanted to be an artist. After spending two years at Agnes Scott, she fulfilled that wish by studying painting in New York, remaining there after completing her art course to become a fashion illustrator for *Woman's Wear Daily* and *The New York Times*. One night she attended a party where she happened to meet fellow Georgian, Bob Turner, a Citadel graduate then working for Morgan's Guarantee Trust. These two Southerners—whose hometowns were twenty-five miles apart—had not known each other previously. But hailing from similar backgrounds in the fast paced urban commercial world, they were drawn together. Their friendship turned into romance and they married in 1936. For a few years afterward, they remained in New York, but when their sons—Robert Pate Jr. (R.P.) and Tom—came along they decided to return to their roots. Marshallville was the logical choice because of Louise's family interests. Bob Turner kept up his wife's family tradition by serving as owner and operator of the family store, while supervising his own agricultural interests and carrying out his duties as Director of the Citizen's Bank of Marshallville.

Louise devoted her spare time to playing the piano and developing her painting skills. A very talented and diversified woman, Louise's prolific artistic output ran on two separate courses. The first entailed fulfilling commissions for precise watercolors of flowers, primarily the magnolias and camellias that grew around their Marshallville home. These were exhibited and sold all over the nation, awarding her the title: "Flower Lady of Marshallville." Her second artistic endeavor involved painting portraits. For practice she corralled her sons into sitting for her, and her likenesses of them chronicled their growth year by year. But most of all, she loved painting local residents, especially African American children. Their soulful, small faces—some cheerful, some pensive—stare from many of Louise's canvases. She would visit the children's homes where she often had to talk skeptical parents into letting her paint them. On some of these expeditions, Louise would capture scenes of Marshallville, with its quaint railroad station and children playing in the streets.

Although she was several hours away, Louise often visited Atlanta, took occasional classes at the Art Institute, joined the Art

Association and received the brochure describing the European trip. When she discovered that some of her friends were planning to go on the charter, Louise was certain it was right for both of them and she began to work on Bob. At first he was reluctant because late May was a busy time on the farm. But eventually he agreed to go so she would not have to travel alone.

Twelve days before the "Trip to the Louvre" was scheduled to depart, high drama was being staged before a three-judge panel in Atlanta. After many years of failed attempts to topple the century-old county-unit system, another test was before the courts. This time Atlantans felt more optimistic about their chances of success. A retired Atlanta businessman, James O'Hear Sanders, sued the state for denying him rightful representation, asking that the Democratic Party abandon the county-unit system in all state elections. Representing him was Morris B. Abram, the brilliant and outspoken attorney, who had argued the issue before a similar federal tribunal in 1950. Not only was the climate in 1962 more favorable to change than it was twelve years earlier, but the composition of the judicial panel—Judges Elbert Tuttle, Griffin Bell, and Frank Hooper—was more oriented to urban interests.

Shortly before the hearing was scheduled to begin on April 27, Governor Ernest Vandiver and the Georgia Legislature hastily called a special session in hopes of saving the embattled county-unit system. For several days, state lawmakers struggled to come up with a new plan and on the day that the three-judge panel began its hearings the legislature voted to accept a new version that gave the urban areas more unit votes.

But this stop-gap measure was not thorough enough to satisfy the federal tribunal; and on April 28, the judges declared the unit law invalid. While all of this was brewing, the Democratic party quietly agreed to drop the county-unit system from its Fifth District primary. Thus for the first time in recent history Atlanta's Congressional representative would be chosen by the popular vote.

As he prepared to travel abroad, Baxter Jones must have felt a mixture of jubilation and sadness, happy that the unequal voting practices were at last illegal, but regretful that the decision had not come a decade sooner.

CHAPTER 6

❦ Women on Their Own

*A*bout two-thirds of those registered for the trip were women. They were a diverse lot, ranging in age from the early twenties to the upper seventies. Many were friends of Lydia Black and Anne Merritt, and most were typical middle-class Southerners. Well attuned to the expectations of American society during the first two-thirds of the twentieth century, they abided by the rules. After marriage, they were expected to give up all hopes of a career and devote their lives to being creative housewives, attending club meetings, volunteering for charities, gardening, playing bridge, and entertaining. The unwritten manual that directed them would soon be torn to shreds by their daughters and granddaughters. But in 1962, it was daring enough to leave husband and family behind to "go gallivanting" abroad on an excursion devised purely for pleasure and artistic enrichment.

One of these was Sarah (Sally) Lowe Clay Benson, a close friend of Henrietta Ayer. Both women had been widowed while young and had children born two days apart. Sally's background was different from Henrietta's, having grown up as a corn farmer's daughter in Woodstock, Georgia. As the first in her family to have a higher education, she graduated from Hiawassee Women's College in Tennessee. In 1929, she married Alexander Stephens (Steve) Clay III, whose grandfather—the first Alexander Stephens Clay—was a U.S. Senator from Georgia during the 1890s. His uncle was General Lucius Clay, commander of American troops in Germany after World War II, and they grew up like brothers because he was only two or three years older than Steve. Around 1940, the Clays moved into a home on Habersham Road. Steve, a lawyer in the firm of Hirsch, Smith, Kilpatrick & Clay, was also a director of the Fulton National Bank and president of the South East Pipe Line Company.

Sally's comfortable life came to a tragic end in 1945 when Steve attended a meeting at the national headquarters of Gulf Oil in Pittsburgh. As he was returning home aboard a commercial flight, the aircraft encountered a thunderstorm and crashed in West Virginia. All aboard were killed. It was one of several airline tragedies associated with those who signed up for the Art Association tour. At age forty, Sally was left with two children to raise, her daughter (also named Sally) then fifteen and her son Steve Jr. age two.

A few years after her husband's death, Sally married Dr. Marion Benson, chief of staff and head of obstetrics at St Joseph's hospital, then located downtown. It was a happy marriage for them both. Sally met people easily and faced life with a genial, happy outlook. She reveled in preparing gourmet meals, either to share with Marion over a bottle of wine in their kitchen or to entertain her friends at lavish dinner parties. She and Marion had traveled to France several times. So when Lydia Black mentioned that someone was canceling her reservation for the Art Association tour, Sally decided to take her place. The prospect of traveling through Europe with a group of congenial pals was irresistible.

In addition to recruiting Henrietta and Sally, Lydia Black enlisted her own sister-in-law, Anne Black Berry. Her husband Randolph, an executive with Scripto, hailed from Rome, Georgia, where his aunt, Martha Berry, had founded a well-known school for underprivileged children. For several years, Anne and Randy lived in Toronto, while he was Scripto's overseas representative. Besides caring for their two young sons, Randy Jr. and Chris, Anne worked with several organizations dedicated to helping handicapped children. When they returned to Atlanta, she became active in the Cerebral Palsy Society. One of the reasons she decided to go with Lydia on the Art Association tour was that Randy would be in Europe on a business trip and they could return home together on the Air France charter.

A number of other women were leaving their spouses at home. Anna Louise Barry and Beaty Henson were among them and so was Frances Stokes Longino. Her husband, Hinton, was a retired manager of the South Atlantic Division of the Retail Credit Corporation; and her father, Thomas Stokes, had been a founder of Davison's. Known for her wit, beauty, charm, and gracious hospitality, Frances Longino was a member of the public library board and an active participant in the Music Club, the Modern Art Study Group, and the Every Saturday Club, an organization that met weekly to discuss current events, literature, and learning.

One of the most colorful women on the trip was Bessie Pope Therrel, a native of Monticello, Georgia. A flamboyant, middle-aged blonde, she was married to Malcom Therrel, a successful

Atlanta contractor. Her passions ranged from entertaining to redecorating their home with black and white zebra-skin furniture and bright-red carpets. Her neighbor Paul Seydel, remembers that she owned at least fifteen cats, which she frequently tried in vain to pawn off on his then-wife, Helen. And Bessie loved to dance. *Atlanta Constitution* columnist, Kathryn Grayburn, noted that Bessie and her close friend Edith Sorrow, wife of publisher Fred Sorrow, were devotees of "the Twist" when it became a craze in the late '50s. Both Bessie and Edith were volunteers at the Atlanta Art Association's Coach House, so when Anne Merritt made her announcement about the European tour, they readily signed up.

Frances Havens Beers was also happy to be traveling with friends. A native of Dallas, Texas, she and her widowed mother moved to Atlanta in 1929. After attending Connecticut College, Frances married prominent local contractor Billy Beers in 1936 and they had two daughters, Marie and Nancy. But the marriage failed, and by 1962, she was divorced. Always interested in the arts, Frances was an active member of the Atlanta Art Association, with a special interest in the furniture collection. "She was absolutely delightful, delicate, small, dark," recalled her friend, Doris Lockerman, "pretty as she could be, really lovely. . . vivid, beautiful, and very bright." The trip to Europe seemed to be the perfect tonic for Frances Beers and she was excited about going.

Mary Ansley Howland was also a recent divorcee. Born in Decatur in 1909, she was the middle child and only daughter of Dr. Wiley Shorter Ansley. Mary attended Agnes Scott and in 1932 married William Slocum Howland, a Princeton graduate who came to Atlanta as a cub reporter at the *Atlanta Journal*. After their marriage, William Howland was an editor in Nashville and Winston Salem, before returning to Atlanta in 1939 to open the first Southeastern bureau for *Time*.

While living in Nashville, the Howlands had a daughter, Annesley, born in 1935. Their son, Slocum (whose godmother was Margaret Mitchell) came along in 1940 and Edith arrived in 1948. Their West Wesley Road home was large enough to contain a barn, an ample garden, and space for Slocum to keep a horse. They joined the Piedmont Driving Club and Mary belonged to the Junior League, volunteering often at their Atlanta Speech School. A slight, dark-haired beauty, Mary was a good athlete and thrived during the family's summers in Deer Isle, Maine. In 1957, William Howland left *Time* to take a public relations job at the University of Miami. During her stay there, Mary developed an interest in the arts and became a docent at Viscaya, the John Deere estate then serving as the Dade County Art Museum.

But life in Florida proved to be difficult, and in 1960 she moved back to Decatur to live with her brother, Dr. Robert Ansley, and shortly afterwards she and Bill divorced. Her daughter, Annesley was then married and living in Atlanta; Slocum was in college at the University of North Carolina; and Edith was finishing high school. A trip to Europe with friends seemed like a good way to deal with her divorce, so like several other women in a similar situation, Mary signed up for the Art Association tour.

Eighteen of the women aboard the Air France charter were touring with family members, some were sisters or sisters-in-law, some cousins, some mothers and daughters. Dorothy Brine, a researcher at Georgia Tech, was traveling with her mother, May, a widow who had worked at Georgia Power where her husband had been an official. The two women had long planned to see the monuments of Europe and at last their dream was about to come true.

Clementina Marks MacPherson from Montgomery, Alabama, announced that she would treat her two daughters—Lee Virgin and Frances Hill—to the European excursion, but their husbands would have to pay their own way if they wanted to come along. Under this mandate, Frank Virgin decided to remain in Atlanta and his brother-in-law, Inge Hill, chose to stay in Montgomery. Clementina, whose granddaughter described her as "an elegant if slightly formidable woman," was the widow of a Montgomery banker. A self-proclaimed arbiter of fashion, interior decorating, landscaping, and just about any subject that needed an opinion, Clementina felt obligated to put her stamp of approval on everything from dresses to garden design.

Eight years separated Clementina's two daughters, but despite their age difference they remained close. From her protected Montgomery background, Lee attended Sweetbriar College for a year before transferring to Smith. After receiving her BA, she studied journalism at Columbia University and subsequently worked as a writer in New York. Frances had married a soldier stationed in Alabama, but when he was killed fighting in France, she went to live with Lee in New York and attend the Finch School.

Lee knew Frank Virgin in Montgomery, and after the war ended, they married; two years later Frances married William Inge Hill. Lee and Frank settled in Atlanta, where he worked in the cotton business and she cared for their two children: Frank, born in 1948, and Clementina (called Clement), born three years later. Frances's children Inge and Lee came along in 1949 and 1952. Both Lee Virgin and Frances Hill were avid readers and both were outgoing and generous, making friends easily and laughing frequently. And they shared their mother's love of gardening and opera. So it was a compatible threesome that prepared to go abroad in May 1962.

Elizabeth (Betsy) Bevington was also traveling with her mother, Dell White Rickey. Born in Richmond, Betsy moved with her parents to Milwaukee when she was ten. She went back east to attend Wellesley College where she majored in psychology. In her junior year, mutual friends introduced her to Milton Bevington, an M.I.T. graduate from Nashville, Tennessee, then attending Harvard Business School. They fell in love and married in 1951, shortly after both graduated. For slightly more than four years, they lived in the Boston area where Milton worked as an assistant superintendent of a chemical plant and Betsy devoted herself to their three sons, Milton Jr., Rickey, and Peter. In the mid-fifties, Milton took a job for Westinghouse's air conditioning division in Staunton, Virginia.

In the meantime, the Rickey's had moved from Milwaukee to Atlanta, and when Betsy and Milton visited them, they were overwhelmed with the beauty of the city, especially the residential section. The lure of Atlanta converged with Milton's interest in restructuring his department, and he spent a spring weekend developing a new business plan, sold his boss on the idea, and not long afterward moved to Atlanta. Betsy, a lively, attractive brunette, had always loved the arts, so shortly after moving to Atlanta she began attending art classes and serving as a docent at the Art Association.

Since her college days, the Rickeys had promised Betsy a trip to Europe. Their younger daughter, Nancy, had traveled abroad with her mother a few years earlier, but with three children, Betsy could never find time to make the trip. Her father retired in 1959 and he and his wife bought a working orange grove in Winter Park, Florida. Since the three Bevington boys were in school, it became easier for Betsy to take the promised trip, which she and her parents began planning. Then in January 1962, her father died suddenly. A few months later, when Betsy learned about the Art Association tour, she realized this was her chance. Not only would the trip be a comfortable and inexpensive way to see Europe, but it would provide a happy distraction to help her mother heal from her recent bereavement.

There were several other women traveling with friends and relatives. Lillie Minier, an active member of the Art Association's Women's Committee, was with her sister Theodosia Barnett of Tampa, Florida. Elizabeth Blair, the widow of a physician and former Marietta mayor, was traveling with her friend Virginia Cowan, whose late husband had been the president of the Georgia Marble Company. Virginia's niece Margherretta Luty— director of the school of psychiatric nursing at the University of Pennsylvania Hospital—was also going with them.

A number of the women traveling on the Air France charter were widows in their sixties, who felt secure traveling with a group organized by the local museum. Mildred Hodges Dilts, an energetic little woman born in Fort Smith, Arkansas, was going to Europe for the first time. Her husband, Bill, had died a few years earlier and she was at loose ends. They had met in Dallas, Texas when he was an Army veteran recently returned from serving overseas in World War I. At the time of their marriage, he was a traveling representative of Vanity Fair Mills. They lived in Dallas until after their son William Jr. was born, but the family moved frequently to various locations around the Southeast because of Bill's job. A second son, Jerry, was born in Birmingham, shortly before they settled in Atlanta around 1936. By then Bill Sr. had become a district manager and then a vice president of Vanity Fair. Mildred poured her talents into cultivating flowers and participating in garden club activities. Her daughter-in-law remembers that she was a very talented woman with an artistic eye, who would tackle anything whether it was an elaborate flower arrangement or a room needing a coat of paint.

When Mildred heard about the Art Association trip, she and

her good friend, Allee Sutton Tidmore, decided to go because both of them had long wanted to travel in Europe. The two women were quite similar. Both loved gardening and enjoyed working with neighborhood garden clubs. Like Mildred, Allee was not a native Atlantan, having come to the state capital from Emanuel County. After graduating from Georgia State College for Women in Milledgeville, she entered nursing school at Piedmont Hospital, but gave up the idea of a career after she married Dr. Thomas Lee Tidmore in 1925. They had three children, a daughter, Teresa, and two younger sons, Tom and Bill. After her husband died, Allee got her real-estate license and became an agent for the Harry Norman agency.

Several doctors' widows also signed up. Emily Webster Pruitt grew up in Cordele, Georgia. Trained as a laboratory technician at the University of Pennsylvania, she took a job at Emory University Hospital. While working there, she met her husband, Atlanta physician Dr. Marion C. Pruitt. Emily was always involved in the arts, both as an amateur painter and as an interested connoisseur. After her husband's death in 1957, she began traveling in Europe to view the masterpieces first hand. This trip with the Art Association would give her the chance to travel with friends and see some of her favorite places. Annette Snelson Payne, whose late husband, Dr. Harvey Payne, was a dentist, decided to travel with the group. Five years earlier, Annette and Harvey—a faculty member of the Emory University Dental School and president of the Southern Society of Orthodontists and the Georgia Dental Association—had attended a dental convention in Rome.

Ruby Stow had been a widow for twelve years. Always friendly and outgoing, Ruby loved to meet people and was certain to make friends on the tour. She came from Concord, a rural outpost in south Georgia, where she was born in 1903. After her father died, her mother, Maybelle Robertson, turned their Concord house into a hotel in order to support her family. Traveling businessmen would time their journeys so they could get off the train and take their midday meal at Miss Maybelle's.

When her two daughters finished high school, Maybelle sold the hotel and moved to Decatur, and Ruby found work selling umbrellas at Rich's. Roy Stow, a widower with a small son, soon began courting her. After their marriage in 1925, they moved to Jacksonville, Florida, where he was a field representative for a building supply company. An inveterate gardener, Ruby divided her time between taking care of the kids—Roy Jr. (her step-son) and her own two children, Jim and Jane—tending her flowers, and working with the P.T.A. They returned to Atlanta in 1945, and settled in a home near Emory. The two boys were in the service and Jane entered Druid Hills High School as a senior.

Five years after their move, Roy died, leaving Ruby as an unprepared widow. An angular, kind-hearted woman, she found solace in volunteering to drive handicapped children for Aidmore (later Scottish-Rite) Hospital. By then Jane had graduated from the University of Georgia and was living in Cartersville with her husband, Bill Greene, and their three sons.

Although Ruby had traveled with Roy around the United States and had once gone with friends to Canada, she had never been to Europe. Jane encouraged her to go, but a few weeks prior to the trip, she became nervous. A few years earlier she had surgery to remove a kidney, and she heard that drinking water in strange countries was dangerous. To placate those apprehensions, her doctor prescribed capsules to dissolve in the water. Then she began to worry about insurance. Her representative said that her policy was invalid for chartered flights, so she purchased an additional policy in case of an accident. This prospect caused additional fears. Europe was so far away, flying was so dangerous. Even Jane's reassurances that everything would be fine did little to assuage her fears. Yet in the end she agreed tentatively to take the tour.

Katherine Bleckley—one of several career women registered for the Air France charter—was also reluctant about going. Shortly before her departure, she told her sister-in-law that she wished she could get out of the Art Association trip and travel instead on an English Speaking Union tour. But she was not one to renege on a promise, and so she went along with her original plans. In 1962, "Miss Katherine," as everyone called her, was recently retired from a long career of service to the state. Her grandfather, Logan Edwin Bleckley, had been chief justice of the state supreme court and one of the most famous Georgians of his day, memorialized as a poet and scholar when he died in 1907. His son, Logan A. Bleckley received his law degree from the University of Georgia and was clerk of the Georgia Court of Appeals for thirty-one years. He married Marion Cooper Wallace, whose family owned a plantation near Athens, and they had twins, Katherine and Logan Jr., born in 1892.

Katherine followed in the family tradition. Tall, sturdy, and resolute, she played volleyball at Girls High and continued to enjoy the game for years. After receiving a BA from the University of Georgia in 1918, she went to work as a staff member of the American Red Cross. Eight years later, she joined her father as chief deputy clerk for the state court of appeals. Then in 1934, she was chosen to be the first female Clerk of the Georgia Supreme Court, one of only two women in the United States to hold that position. It carried a great deal of responsibility, from providing the dockets to organizing and managing daily operations of the court. During her twenty-eight year tenure, Katherine Bleckley's name appeared on the certificate of every lawyer who passed the Georgia Bar. For her service, she received the "Woman of the Year in the Professions" award in 1957.

Miss Katherine lived in the Victorian house on Piedmont Avenue that had been purchased by her parents in 1912. Her brother Logan, Jr. moved away for awhile after his marriage, but shortly after their father died he brought his wife and son back to the family home. Katherine's nephew Logan III, who still lives in the house, remembers his aunt returning so exhausted from work that she had to lie down before dinner.

In the early '40s, Katherine and her co-worker Ella Thornton founded the local chapter of the English Speaking Union, an organization devoted to promoting Anglo-American friendship, dispensing scholarships, offering hospitality to visiting Britons, presenting lectures, and, of course, holding teas. During World War II, she arranged for RAF pilots training at Fort Benning to spend weekends in Atlanta homes. For that and other services to England, Queen Elizabeth II awarded her the Order of the British Empire. Ella Thornton later said that Miss Katherine virtually ran the 750-member organization single handedly and held meetings in her Victorian living room because the Union had no permanent office space. It was the chance to return once more to England that persuaded Miss Katherine to go ahead with plans to take the Art Association tour. She would visit friends in Yorkshire for a while, before traveling to Austria with her cousin, Margaret Nutting, a recently retired legal secretary.

Ruth Morris was another career woman on the tour. Like Katherine Bleckley, she never married and devoted herself entirely to her rewarding job. Until 1961, she had been a home-lighting specialist at the Georgia Power Company, a firm which she joined in 1918 and where she remained for the rest of her career. Her work in designing residential lighting was highly regarded in the industry. A year before her retirement, Morris received a recognition award from the Atlanta Residence Lighting Forum, an organization she had founded in 1944. Without her challenging job, she was restless. The European trip might broaden her horizons and introduce her to new ways to direct her life.

Helen Camp Richardson also had a rewarding career. For forty-two years she had taught biology at Bass High (and formerly Junior High) School before her retirement three years earlier. She signed up for the Air France charter because she planned to travel with her niece and ward whose husband was stationed in Europe. Her own husband, William, a retired engineer, was remaining at home. Emily Bartholomai, who had recently retired from the Georgia Department of Health after working there for twenty years, rewarded herself with a trip to Europe, leaving her husband Carl, an entomologist at Fort McPherson, behind. Anna Mulcahy was also anxiously awaiting her getaway. For the past twenty years she had worked as an office manager for Weideman Singleton and saved her money for such a trip.

Louise Loomis was one of the youngest women on the chartered flight. She had recently graduated cum laude from the University of North Carolina at Chapel Hill and had spent the past year as a provisional member of the Junior League, which meant volunteering for charities. In addition to working at the Atlanta Art Association and Humane Society, she helped as a playground director for poor, black children, a bold pursuit in still-segregated Atlanta. Louise had been accepted in the graduate department of sociology at Washington University in St. Louis and was preparing to enter in the fall of '62. Having a year off would allow her to spend time with her grandparents, Mr. and Mrs. Thomas Kenan, who had raised her and her brother, Gregg, since their mother died when Louise was born. Although she had been to Europe once before, Louise was anxious to return. Then a few weeks before the Air France charter was scheduled to depart, her grandfather died. Louise was devastated. She felt she should stay home to help her grandmother, but both Gregg and Mrs. Kenan insisted that the trip would provide a good break before she entered graduate school in the fall. So despite her mixed feelings, she reluctantly decided to go.

These women all grew up in relative comfort. Most had an advanced education beyond high school, the majority having graduated from college. In the mid-twentieth-century South, they represented the upper echelon of privilege with all the advantages. Touring Europe—which was still a novelty for most Americans—carried a sense of high adventure. Adhering to convictions of the time, most believed that no education was complete without exposure to European monuments and culture, a pleasurable ritual guaranteed to turn provincial Southerners into urbane sophisticates.

CHAPTER 7

≋ Commitment to the Arts

Within twenty-four hours of his scheduled departure on the Art Association tour, Del Paige attended two meetings that promised significant changes in the arts of Atlanta. His first appearance on Tuesday, May 8, was before the Joint Atlanta-Fulton County Bond Commission, where as chairman of the mayor's Cultural Needs Committee, Paige was asking for the upcoming bond referendum to set aside $3 million of the proposed allocation for constructing a fine arts center. The project was organized with cooperation from the Atlanta Arts Festival, which agreed to help launch the publicity.

The 1962 Arts Festival—held for one week each May in Piedmont Park—was scheduled to begin several days after the Art Association tour departed for France. It constituted the city's only combined presentation of the visual and performing arts. On a first-come, first-serve basis, local artists leased flats that stretched across the red clay paths, producing a potpourri of quality and styles heightened by a carnival atmosphere. A more polished show filled the old stone bathhouse next to the lake, with artwork chosen by a jury. The *piece de resistance* was the ongoing schedule of performances on a makeshift stage across from the bathhouse, where local dance groups, chamber music quartets, theatrical outfits, and folk singers performed periodically throughout the afternoon and evening.

For the past two years, Atlantans had been working on a plan for providing a permanent home for the city's performing arts. The prime mover was none other than Coca-Cola magnate, Robert W. Woodruff, working quietly behind the scenes. For quite awhile, he had wanted to do something spectacular for the city, and as a key member of the mayor's advisory power structure, he knew Atlanta was embarrassingly under funded in its cultural offerings. Woodruff, however, had little knowledge of the arts and so to investigate the matter, he hired Dr. Philip Weltner, the former president of Oglethorpe University, to head his family's charitable foundation.

One of Weltner's most cherished dreams was creating a cultural center in a park-like setting. The Arts Festival's success in Piedmont Park indicated that the publicly owned site would be ideal. With this in mind, Woodruff informed Ivan Allen that his foundation would put up $4 million if the city could raise matching funds through a bond referendum. One major stipulation was that Woodruff's name not be connected with the gift. Therefore, the Arts Festival and the city's Cultural Needs Committee—chaired by Del Paige—would act as public sponsors of the plan, which specified the construction of a large concert hall and theater, a series of galleries and pergolas for revolving exhibitions, an ice skating rink, a crystal-palace-style greenhouse, and several restaurants.

The Arts Festival dispersed volunteers to circulate petitions, in hopes that a large number of signatures would convince the bond commission that the $7 million project had public support. As a liaison between the city and the arts community, Del Paige was faced with two problems. Not only would matching public funds for the park project be difficult to acquire, but he realized that many members of the Art Association board would vote against a rival venture. To make matters worse, the fact that the donor remained anonymous opened a Pandora's box of speculation about his identity. Nevertheless, Paige expressed confidence that the ballot would include a segment earmarked to prepare Piedmont Park for a cultural center. A decision on the matter would not come until the end of the month, and by that time, he would be in Europe.

Paige left the bond commission hearing on May 8 and put on his Art Association hat. The executive committee had scheduled a meeting just prior to his departure to discuss the Engelhardt plan. With little prodding, the committee approved recommendations for a major school renovation, employment of a qualified director for the museum, and hiring of a professional overseer for the entire institution. It was a big and expensive step to take, and the trustees considered their responsibilities earnestly.

Four trustees of the Art Association—Sidney Wien, Raiford Ragsdale, Del Paige, and Ruth McMillan—were preparing to travel on the Air France charter along with a very diverse assortment of individuals deeply involved in some aspect of the arts. If anything could be called a common denominator, it was their commitment to life's "finer things." Sidney Wien, a retired real estate executive, was a leading member of the Art Association board. Born in New York City in 1902, he attended public schools and studied accounting at the Pratt Institute. His father,

Joseph Wien, had immigrated from Russia as a teen-ager, arriving in New York with no money, no knowledge of the English language, and no idea about American customs. Beginning as a salesman in a clothing store, he rose in the profession and within a couple of years was able to purchase a factory that manufactured women's shirtwaists. At age twenty-two, he became a naturalized citizen and shortly afterwards married Bessie Meyers. During the next two decades, they had five sons and a daughter.

In 1914, Joe Wien left the shirtwaist business and began manufacturing silks in Paterson, New Jersey, soon opening a second mill in Bethlehem, Pennsylvania. Sidney worked with his father at their Paterson headquarters until 1931. Subsequently he left New York, and after a short stint in California, ended up in Miami. One day while walking on the beach, he met twenty-year-old Ellen Michelson, who was in Miami vacationing with her parents. Her father—an immigrant from Latvia—was a successful Baltimore cigar manufacturer; her highly educated and cultured mother had been born in Germany; and Ellen, born in 1911, was their only child. She graduated from the Peabody Conservatory and was a Phi Beta Kappa graduate of Goucher College. She and Sidney married in 1933, and for their honeymoon traveled around the world. Upon returning to Miami Beach, he joined his friend Paul Prufert in the construction business and together they built office buildings, retail stores, and hotels in the Miami area. During that same time, he and his father-in-law, Jerry Michelson, developed one of the nation's first shopping centers on Lincoln Road.

In the summer of 1942, the Wiens went to Asheville, North Carolina, and fell in love with the area. They bought a large farm and lived there for the next eight years. In 1950, seeking better schools for their daughters, Claire and Joan (nicknamed Toni), they decided to relocate in Atlanta and built a contemporary house on Stratford Road. They joined the Temple and became active in the social life of the community. A slim, soft-spoken man, Sidney Wien was a bright and cultured individual, who enjoyed a good game of golf and had a terrific sense of humor. Ellen was a sparkling, sophisticated woman, whose intelligence, love of music, and warm personality attracted devoted friends. Their interest in art brought them to the Atlanta Art Association. As they began purchasing art for themselves, they also bought for several art museums. Their generosity not only enhanced the holdings of the Atlanta Art Association, but added artworks to the collections of Brandies University in Massachusetts, the Columbus (Georgia) Museum, and New York's Whitney Museum of American Art.

Sidney was on the acquisitions committee of the High Museum, and contributed money periodically toward enhancing their holdings. A large part of the Wien's own collection—as well as the works they donated to museums—came from living artists, with whom the couple developed personal friendships. Their contributions to the Atlanta Art Association in 1961 and 1962 included a watercolor by the Massachusetts painter John Whorf, prints by the well-known New York sculptor Chaim Gross, a bronze sculpture by Albert Vrana of Miami, a drawing by African-American artist Herman Bailey, and paintings by Atlantans Joseph Perrin and George Beattie. In the days when the High Museum had a paucity of original artworks, Sidney and Ellen Wien were listed among the institution's principal donors.

In 1962, Sidney and Ellen decided to sign up for the Air France chartered flight so they could travel through Europe looking for artwork and introduce Toni to some of their favorite places. She had followed her sister to Wellesley College, where she majored in Art History, and was then working for a publishing firm in New York City. An enthusiastic, bright, twenty-three-year-old woman, Toni was enjoying her independence, her job, her friends, and was about to become engaged. All three Wiens looked forward to a leisurely three-week ramble through France and Italy.

Among others who signed up for the trip were both professional and amateur artists. All were deeply committed to beautifying their own world; and in that realm, all had their own private reasons for traveling abroad. For a talented young man named William David Cogland, it was the inexpensive fare that enticed him to sign up for the chartered flight. Born on a tenant farm in Grady County, Georgia in 1935, David was the youngest of three children. In the early 1940s, the family moved to southeast Atlanta. After graduating from Roosevelt High School in the early '50s, David—whose burning passion was drawing and painting—won a scholarship to attend night school at the Atlanta Art Association. During the day, he worked in the display department at Rich's.

In his studio at the rear of his parents' house on Vera Street, Cogland often worked past midnight creating large, colorful abstract paintings. During the 1950s, most Atlantans were unfamiliar with Abstract Expressionism, then the cutting edge in New York galleries. Although family members were supportive, they were completely baffled by his non-objective canvases. Despite Atlanta's provincialism, David was able to impress his teachers and to sell his paintings through local galleries.

To make ends meet, Cogland continued to work at Rich's until he earned enough to start his own display business in the late '50s. While designing window decorations during the day and painting at night, he found time to travel 100 miles by bus once a month to teach art therapy to the inmates at Georgia's mental hospital in Milledgeville. Deciding to work with the criminally insane was both courageous and challenging. Upon first encountering the Milledgeville students, he found them to be listless and disinterested, staring out of the windows instead of paying attention to the lessons. Finally Cogland decided to dismiss the security guards stationed around the room, and gradually the inmates began to respond.

In one of his frequent visits to the High Museum, Cogland learned about the European trip. He had always wanted to go abroad, not only to see the paintings but to find European outlets for his artwork. His friend Doug Davis, a recognized portrait painter, lived in Paris and would guide him toward galleries that might be interested in sponsoring him. So Cogland began saving money for the $388 dollar round-trip fare. He hoped to stay awhile with Doug in Paris and to visit an uncle stationed in Germany.

But Cogland had little time to dwell on planning the trip because he was preparing for a one-man show at the Artist's Associates Gallery on West Peachtree that was due to open a few weeks before his scheduled departure. During the past few years, he had begun experimenting with caseins, using gold leaf in his paintings, and creating a variety of cloth hangings, serigraphs, and mobiles. His most innovative new creations were what he called "color suspensions," layers of stained glass and silver and copper wiring in sculptural shapes. European avant-garde art would provide new ideas for future works, and the galleries of Paris would offer possible new venues. It was a long-anticipated dream that the inexpensive Air France charter was transforming into a reality.

Helen Clark Seydel signed up for different reasons. Recently divorced and seeking a new life, she was anxious to spend a few weeks in Florence to absorb as much as she could. A self-described "army brat," Helen had moved around a lot in her life. Her father, Colonel John Clark, ended his military career at Fort McPherson in Atlanta and decided to remain in the city after his retirement.

Early on, Helen displayed a deep interest in art, a commitment that would absorb her for the rest of her life. After graduating from Washington Seminary, she attended the art school in the old High mansion, and in 1936 she married Paul Seydel Jr., who worked with his uncle, Vassar Woolley, in the chemical manufacturing business.

In the late '30s, Paul and Helen built a house on a twenty-seven acre wooded tract at the end of West Paces Ferry Road, where she could paint in an attached studio surrounded by a tranquil forest. Her paintings, especially the portraits, reflect this serene atmosphere. She herself was ethereal and elegant. Her niece, Susan Seydel Cofer—now a successful Atlanta artist—remembers posing often for her aunt when she was a child. Everything was peaceful and lovely, and to Susan that atmosphere became synonymous with art. Helen even "made a Coca-Cola an artistic experience" by serving it in a crystal glass with cracked ice and a sliver of lemon. And best of all, she began letting Susan paint or draw alongside her.

In 1958, Helen's life changed dramatically when she and Paul divorced. At first she remained in the West Paces Ferry house, but being by herself in the woods was lonesome, so she decided to move into an apartment near Buckhead. Continuing to paint and sell her work locally, Helen occasionally attended Women's Committee meetings at the High Museum. When she learned about the Art Association trip, she decided that travel abroad was just what she needed. She would take the chartered flight and spend three weeks in Florence, where she could have what she hoped would be "a spiritual resurrection."

Paul Barnett was making a spiritual journey of another sort. At age sixty-two, he wanted to follow his passion for Gothic art and architecture, and nowhere were there more beautiful examples than in France. He was writing a book about stained-glass windows and had been there twice before on research ventures.

His editors advised him to return once more before submitting the final manuscript.

The arts were part of Barnett's legacy. His maternal grandfather, Albert Capers Guerry, was a recognized South Carolina painter of the nineteenth century, who traveled around the South painting portraits. On three different occasions, Guerry journeyed to Washington to live in the White House and create likenesses of presidents. Barnett inherited his grandfather's talent and sensitivity toward the arts. Born in Washington, Georgia, in 1900, he always loved to draw and paint. In his youth he even wrote romantic and patriotic poems that were published in local newspapers and in the periodical, *Printer's Ink*.

Barnett divided his education between his aesthete interests and the practical route of engineering, so his life ran on two separate tracks, occasionally intersecting but usually running parallel courses. After about a year at Georgia Tech and a brief stint in the Army during World War I, he ended up studying art in New York City and California. He met and married Olive Logue in DeLand, Florida. They stayed there for a few years before moving to Atlanta, where their two children—a son Paul, Jr. and daughter Guerry—were born.

Although Barnett attended occasional art classes and was constantly working in some artistic pursuit, he spent thirty-six years as an engineer for Southern Bell. Despite his work-a-day job, the arts remained his first love. Architecture, photography, and classical music merged with his interest in drawing and painting. His daughter remembers how he would sit with his eyes closed listening to Bach and Beethoven on the new hi-fi. Every year he designed imaginative Christmas cards—one year, a sketch of their Atlanta home, another, photographs of the children sledding amidst his drawings of pine branches. Each had a poem that relayed a Christmas message and occasionally dispensed family news.

A broad-shouldered man with penetrating eyes and a ready smile, Barnett satisfied his perceptive mind by occasionally taking courses in comparative religion and psychology. He put these interests into practice when he made weekly visits to a friend who had been almost totally debilitated from a stroke. Then Barnett suffered two strokes himself, the last affecting his left side and causing a slight limp. But these minor setbacks never dissuaded him from pursuing his most recent project.

In the late '50s and early '60s, the book on Gothic windows seemed to be expanding into an investigation of French culture. Hoping to strengthen his affected leg for his next research trip, Barnett was determined to walk constantly. His excursions in the French countryside would require enough stamina to set up his old camera with the bellows-style lens and snap frequent photographs of Chartres Cathedral, French people at work and play, and various architectural monuments. After his previous trips, he cropped the pictures and arranged them in albums. In the spring of '62, he had his camera ready again with a supply of film and a notebook to interview people or take notes.

Tom and Charlotte Little were seeking inspiration for their architectural restorations and looking for antiques to furnish them authentically. The Littles were a team; he was a trained architect, she a landscape designer and decorator. Together they enjoyed recreating small corners of seventeenth and eighteenth-century America. Europe would provide a taste of what the first settlers to the United States left behind there and allow them to study the kinds of interiors that the colonists attempted to emulate.

Thomas Goree Little was born in Anniston, Alabama, but his family came to Atlanta when he was a young child. After attending Spring Street Elementary School and Boys High, he received an architectural degree from Georgia Tech in 1935. For two years, he worked for a firm in Columbus, Georgia, and then joined John Russell Pope's architectural practice in New York, with an assignment to help design Washington's Jefferson Memorial and National Gallery. Then in April 1939, he transferred to Williamsburg, Virginia, to participate in restoring the old colonial capital, a far-reaching project funded by the Rockefeller family.

Also working on the Williamsburg restoration was a young woman named Charlotte Henderson. Born in 1919 into a physician's family in Richmond, she had moved with her parents to Williamsburg when she was twelve. After graduating from a local high school, Charlotte spent a short time at Farmville State Teacher's College before transferring to William & Mary. After graduation, she became a hostess for Colonial Williamsburg, taking visitors through the restored houses and working to help plant eighteenth-century-style gardens. She and Tom met amidst the sawdust of the ongoing construction projects. He was helping design and supervise work on Bruton Parish Church and the King's Arms Tavern along with several of the houses and shops. They married in the chapel of William & Mary in September 1940.

Their marriage's idyllic beginning was interrupted when Tom became a Navy Lieutenant and was shipped off to the Pacific. Upon his return, he and Charlotte remained in the Washington area where their first child, Charlotte Patricia (Pat), was born in 1943. Then in 1946, they settled in Atlanta and Tom briefly joined his father's furniture manufacturing and retail business, while Charlotte lectured about Colonial Williamsburg to local women's organizations. Their second child, Thomas G. Little Jr. came along in 1949.

Gradually Tom Little developed his own architectural practice, specializing in reconstruction and restoration of eighteenth-century buildings. Charlotte assisted him in presenting a full package to Atlantans wanting Williamsburg-style homes. He drew carefully researched reproductions of old colonial houses, and she designed the gardens, as well as selected fabrics, wall colors, and authentic furniture. During the 1950s, the Little's Williamsburg-style houses rose around northwest Atlanta. One was their own home built on a steep, wooded lot on East Beechwood Drive.

While designing domestic architecture, Tom—with Charlotte alongside him—became heavily involved in restoring eighteenth-century landmarks under the auspices of the Georgia Historical Commission. Before the days when historical preservation was an accepted practice, the Littles worked tirelessly to save rapidly deteriorating and vanishing structures. Among his renovations were the Washington-Wilkes Museum in Washington, Georgia, the Midway Museum in Midway, the Eagle Tavern in Watkinsville, the print shop at New Echota (the Cherokee village near Calhoun), and the Mackay House in Augusta.

One of their most ambitious and rewarding projects was rebuilding the Redman Thornton House. Under the watchful eye of the Atlanta Art Association's decorative arts curator, James Nonemaker, Tom found a late eighteenth-century structure in the vicinity of Union Point, Georgia. Excluding the addition of a Victorian porch, the house was intact with all the original beaded weatherboards, window sills, sashes, and glass. The brick chimneys on either side remained and indoor plumbing and central heating had never been installed. The Littles supervised disassembly of the Thornton House board by board and brick by brick, with each piece being numbered so the building could be reconstructed at the rear of the Atlanta Art Association property behind the Coach House. Tom's eye for authenticity and Charlotte's knowledge of antiques and eighteenth century plants turned the old Thornton House into a period piece. It was opened to the public in April 1961 with a large party attended by 700 guests.

Even if the Engelhardt report recommended that Thornton House be removed from the Art Association grounds, the Littles were not discouraged. It would find another home somewhere. As they prepared to embark on their journey, Tom and Charlotte felt generally happy and fulfilled.

David Murphy was another architect traveling on the Air France charter. Both he and his wife Betty were native Atlantans. Even though they were acquainted as youngsters growing up in Atlanta, they did not renew the friendship until years later. Elizabeth (Betty) Carver left Atlanta to attend Manhattanville College and returned to graduate from Agnes Scott. Then she married another Atlantan, William (Bill) Grabbe, but their marriage ended tragically when the plane he was piloting crashed early in World War II. This was yet another eerie association with airplane disasters that hung over the Air France charter travelers. After Bill was declared missing and officially dead, Betty returned to Atlanta and later gave birth to their son, Chris.

A few years later, Betty rekindled her friendship with David Murphy and they soon married. After earning a bachelors degree from Georgia Tech and undertaking graduate studies at Cranbrook Academy in Michigan, David went to work with Richard Aeck's architectural firm. He was instrumental in designing the Alexander Coliseum at Georgia Tech, the first large domed structure built in the city, and the football stadium at Grady High School. David and Betty had three children, David Jr., Michael, and Elizabeth. The firm wanted David to investigate architectural sites in several European cities, so the Murphys signed up for the Air France charter. They would leave the group in Paris and meet with them again for the return flight. It would be a great vacation, and having business assignments to fulfill would give their sojourn a purpose.

Another couple anxiously anticipating their getaway were Helen and William (Bill) Cartledge. He was a nightclub owner, she an amateur artist and actress, well-known in local theatrical circles as one of the principal founders of Theatre Atlanta, the city's most popular dramatic group. She had been born Helen Hunt in Dallas, Texas in 1930, the third child of Frania and "Franklin" Hunt. Four years later, when Frania was expecting their fourth child, she discovered that the man she had married in 1925 was none other than the oil tycoon, H.L. (Haroldson Lafayette) Hunt, who had another wife and six children living in Tyler, Texas.

After making this shocking discovery, Frania moved her family from Dallas to New York to Los Angeles, and eventually back to Texas, while she attempted to solve her marital dilemma. Hunt supported her and the children, but made it quite clear that he would never leave his first wife. Finally in 1942, they reached an agreement. Frania would not sue Hunt for bigamy, nor would she publish her story; he would give her a settlement and set up a trust for each of the four children. Shortly after she signed the agreement, Frania married John Lee, an employee of the Hunt Oil Company and moved to Atlanta. Helen was then twelve. Lee adopted all four children and gave them his name. Shortly after their marriage, he went into the military and remained a shadowy figure in the children's lives until Frania divorced him in 1957.

With a great deal of money to spend, Frania Lee became a prominent figure in Atlanta society. She renovated a large colonial manor northwest of Atlanta called "Flowerland," which she later donated to the Roman Catholic Archdiocese for use as a school known as the D'Youville Academy. Meanwhile in 1955, Hunt's first wife died and he married his secretary, Ruth Ray Wright, by whom he had fathered four more children—bringing the total of his known offspring to fourteen.

As Helen Lee matured, she seemed to possess the best attributes of both parents. Statuesque, blonde, and elegant, she had her father's spunk and her mother's genuine interest in people. Hunt remained a presence in her life. She was, in fact, said to have been his favorite in the second family. After graduating from Marymount College in Tarrytown, New York, she spent three years in Manhattan studying acting, designing sets, and directing. But the hustle of Broadway was too harrowing and she returned to Atlanta, where she became involved in local theater and took painting classes at the Art Association.

Her former sister-in-law remembers her as a very creative person who could paint, act, and play the piano. She was always dignified and commanding, in fact, "queenly," a role she fit into easily when playing Queen of the May in a theatrical production at Marymount College. In 1956, she married William Cartledge, a native of Charlotte, North Carolina, who owned and managed the El Morocco Supper Club, located in a small apartment building on Peachtree. Unlike many other nightclub owners, Bill Cartledge was a clean-cut guy, who stayed away from drinking and gambling.

A year after their marriage, three theatrical groups joined together to form Theatre Atlanta. Helen became active in the organization and in 1961 founded the Women's Guild to serve as the theatre's fundraising and publicity arm. "Helen would do just about anything in a pinch for the theater," her mother later recalled. In addition to acting and designing sets, she went to great lengths to procure donations in any form, whether cash, costumes, or stage props. Helen and Bill bought a house in

Ansley Park and shortly afterward, Frania bought a house nearby. Then in 1958, they had a son, Ronald, whom they called "Ronny." It would soon be time for him to start school and Helen became interested in the Montessori system, inspiring her brother, Hugh, and his then-wife in bringing those independent schools to the greater Atlanta area.

During those years, she devoted a great deal of time to working for Theatre Atlanta, continuing to dabble in art, and teaching drama at the D'Youville Academy. The Cartledges signed up for the chartered plane to Paris because they had long wanted to visit Greece. Ronny would be under Frania's supervision while they were away. At that time, only rumors suggested that Helen's father was H.L. Hunt and many years would elapse before Atlantans learned the full story.

In addition to Julia Jones and Louise Turner, there were a few other amateur artists planning to embark on the Art Association tour. One was Mary Louise (Puddin) Bealer Humphries, who grew up in Ansley Park and graduated from Agnes Scott College in 1946. Although she was high-spirited and fun-loving, Puddin was serious about her painting, exhibiting at local galleries and occasionally selling her work. Dolly Brooks, from Griffin, Georgia—a woman in her mid- sixties—was also serious about painting. She had once been an art student in Paris and studied in New York with the Chinese-American watercolorist Dong Kingman.

When she signed up for the Art Association tour, Mary Louise Perkins was working as a decorator and color consultant for her husband's architectural firm. In 1931, she had been the first woman to receive a bachelors degree in the visual arts from the University of Georgia. Mary Scott (Molly) Newcomb Bull was another amateur artist going on the chartered flight. She was traveling with her brother, Robert Newcomb, her son Frederick, his wife, and two teen-aged granddaughters. She frequently painted family portraits, especially of her son and grandchildren. As the Art Association tour prepared to leave, Del Paige—exhausted from his two days of meetings to determine Atlanta's artistic future—was figuring out ways to communicate from Europe with members of the Cultural Needs Committee to learn if the Piedmont Park project would be included in the upcoming bond referendum. It was certainly not a convenient time for the most visible link between the Art Association and the proposed cultural center to be spending three weeks abroad.

PART II

Traveling Abroad

CHAPTER 8:

❧ *The Departure*

*T*he new $13,000,000 terminal at the Atlanta Airport cele-
brated its first birthday a few days before the Art
Association tour was scheduled to depart for Europe.
The new glazed-blue-metal and glass building with its scalloped
portico and eight-story tower was considered extremely modern
and, therefore, controversial when it opened in 1961. As people
entered the front doors, they felt dwarfed by the large two-story
atrium decorated with artificial plants and trees draped with
Spanish moss. Above their heads whirled a gold and enameled
mobile by Atlanta artist, Julian Harris, which consisted of metal
arrows tipped with red airplanes dangling around a stylized
phoenix. It was unquestionably the most talked-about sculpture
in the city because critics argued that taxpayers should not have
to pay $35,000 for an unfathomable piece of art.

At midday on May 9, 1962, the new terminal was abuzz with excited chatter. The long-anticipated "Trip to the Louvre" was finally underway. Groups of people were inching toward the Air France desk, many looking tired and overwrought from the Metropolitan Opera's annual visit to the Fox Theater.

Many of the women leaving on May 9 were not only attending the operas and accompanying balls at the Capital City and Piedmont Driving Clubs, but they were busy with their duties as members of the Junior League, principal sponsor of the performances. If they weren't handing out programs and acting as ushers at the Fox, they were attending opera-related functions. One of these was a luncheon of the Opera Guild at the Driving Club on May 4. Julia Jones, as president of that organization, sat at the head table in the club's ballroom decorated with a Viennese theme inspired by *Cossi Fan Tutte.*

Before the frenetic pace of opera week, there were a series of bon voyage parties, in which friends and family presented useful gifts to the travelers. Del and Winifred Paige were feted several times, beginning with a luncheon at the Cherokee Club on April 12, followed several weeks later by another celebration at the Coach House. Lucy Candler's sewing club gave a morning coffee in her honor on the Friday before their Wednesday departure. Her husband, Ezekiel (Zeke), was a descendant of the famous Candler family that founded Coca-Cola. He, in fact, had been a long-time employee of Coke, having first served them in his home town of Dallas, Texas. Prominent in Atlanta society, Lucy Candler had graduated from Wesleyan College and was active in numerous charitable organizations.

A few weeks before the group was scheduled to depart, Ruby Adair held a bon voyage luncheon for members of her garden club and other friends going on the Art Association tour. Like Ruby, most were widows in their sixties. Charles A. Adair had passed away about a year earlier and Ruby was still struggling with getting her life back together. When Mildred Dilts, Beaty Henson, Frances Longino, Annette Payne, Raiford Ragsdale, and a few others assembled for lunch at the Capitol City Club, they talked excitedly about the planned trip. In the course of their conversation, they began insisting that their hostess join them. Ruby was tempted even though she had traveled in Europe before.

That evening she contacted her brother, Wesley Martin, and asked his opinion. Martin and his sister were very close, although she was fourteen years older. He was an adolescent when their mother died and Ruby took him into her home. Later he worked with his brother-in-law at C.A. Adair & Company, and after Charles retired he ran the construction firm. With no children of her own, Ruby considered the Martin kids her grandchildren, and since Charles's death she depended more and more on her brother's advice. He wholeheartedly endorsed her taking the trip to Europe, seeing it as a way for Ruby to forget her recent loss and enjoy touring with her friends. With the help of Anne Merritt and others, Ruby secured the reservation and hastily prepared for the trip.

On the afternoon of Sunday, May 6, Frania Lee held an open house at her Ansley Park home to honor her daughter and son-in-law, Helen and Bill Cartledge. This was just one of Helen's appearances during the busy days before her departure. As chairman of the Woman's Guild of Theatre Atlanta, she presided over a luncheon at the Cherokee Town Club the day before her departure and was so rushed she appeared at the lectern with wet hair. But despite her impossible schedule, Helen had to attend. Not only did she announce that their next season would begin in a new Fifteenth Street location, but Helen also told the organization that she was presenting George Goodwin, the president of Theatre Atlanta, a check for $500 from her most recent fund raising efforts.

That same Tuesday, Ruth McMillan played a significant role at a different luncheon. As outgoing president of the Women's Committee of the Atlanta Art Association, she presented a check for $32,342 to Del Paige. It constituted the proceeds from the last flea market. In the past year, she boasted, the Women's Committee had contributed $45,000 toward supporting the museum and art school, the largest amount ever raised by her team of volunteers.

Shortly before the meeting, Ruth McMillan confessed to her friend Cecile Goodhart that she didn't want to travel to Europe on this trip. Having served for a year as Women's Committee president, she was so tired that she preferred to spend the three weeks resting at home. But her obligations to the association and her instrumental part in organizing the tour meant she was duty-bound to travel. She was not alone in her apprehensions. Carroll Young told her daughter that she was already homesick before they even left Atlanta and regretted that the magnolias would bloom while she was away. In fact, she confessed, "the only place I want to be is with you and your family." Ruby Stow remained so nervous about the trip that her daughter, Jane Greene, was afraid she would change her mind at the last minute. But after friends took her to the plane, they called Jane to assure her that Ruby seemed relaxed and delighted to be going.

Younger children were not encouraging their parents to go. Rather they were begging them to stay home. In Montgomery, Inge Hill was uneasy about his mother traveling so far away. Such fears are common when parents leave home for a prolonged period, but there are numerous memories of dire premonitions connected with the Atlanta Art Association tourists. Inge's fears may have been triggered by his mother's own uneasiness because

Frances Hill felt so sick a week before her departure that she announced that she might have to stay home. However, when her doctor, Jane Day, examined her, she found nothing wrong and told Frances she should plan to go. Frances, therefore, went about packing so she could travel with her mother and sister.

Nina Crimm remembers watching from the kitchen window on May 9, as her mother walked down the driveway in her high-heeled shoes, bound for Peachtree Road. One of her father, Reuben's, law partners was driving them to the airport, and Jan was taking the bus to his office. Nina had urged her parents not to take the trip, certain they would never return. Apparently Reuben had misgivings, too. Although he and Jan traveled together on a regular basis, this time he took special precautions. En route to the airport, he instructed his partner to rewrite their will to make his sister, Rosalene, the children's guardian, insuring they could stay together in Atlanta and not have to be separated and sent to live in the homes of different relatives.

Another lawyer traveling with the group, Arnold Kaye, also took last-minute precautions. Not only had he updated his will, but he and Gladys made sure that her sister and brother-in-law, Audrey and Jake Goldstein, would look after their two boys in case anything happened. Dr. Chris McLoughlin also made last-minute changes. He wrote a letter instructing his will be altered and enclosed it in an envelope marked: "To be opened in the event that we do not return." Perhaps the most dramatic forewarning came from the artist David Cogland. While talking on the phone, it was his habit to doodle on a scratch pad. A day or two before the Art Association tour was scheduled to depart, he drew an airplane nose down and in flames.

But the crowd gathering at the Atlanta Airport showed few signs of anxiety. The passengers in line at the Air France ticket counter were chatting excitedly as they waited to check their baggage. After the travelers showed their tickets and passports, a representative of the airline gave each of them a large name tag. Many had arrived several hours early so they could have lunch in the Passport restaurant upstairs overlooking the field. The publicity and hype surrounding the first-ever tour tailored for an Atlanta cultural organization brought an entourage of relatives and acquaintances to the terminal to bid the Art Association group farewell. Ivan and Louise Allen were there to tell their friends goodbye and act as official emissaries from City Hall. Aubrey Morris of WSB and several other local media personnel were also on hand, anxious to record the event that had received so much local attention.

The entire Bull family—Fred, his wife Barbara, their daughters Betsy and Ellen, Fred's mother Mary, and her brother Robert Newcomb—were all there together. So were the many women traveling with friends, relatives, or family members. Augusta Streyer Miller, whose late husband, an insurance agent, had been a member of the Piedmont Driving Club, was talking excitedly with her friends. Clementina MacPherson was in the waiting room with her two daughters, Lee Virgin and Frances Hill; Katherine Bleckley and her cousin Margaret Nutting were together. Catherine Mitchell was talking with friends about the operas, especially the supper party at the Capital City Club where she hosted a table. Active both in the Opera Guild and the Art Association, Catherine was eager to go abroad, partially because she planned to meet up with her close friends, the Vol T. Blacknall's, who had left several weeks earlier to tour Ireland, Scotland and England.

Ready for a vacation after the hectic pace of opera week, members of the Old Atlanta bunch were clustered together anticipating the trip with glee. Others seemed to know few people and were quietly conversing with each other. Dr. Roy Bixler, a retired professor, college administrator, and writer, was standing with his wife Ella, a professor of nursing. They had met years earlier while both were in graduate school at Columbia University in New York. Roy taught for a while at the University of Chicago before becoming the Registrar at Drake University in Iowa. After his retirement eight years earlier, they came to Atlanta so Ella could be near the home base for the Southern Regional Board on Nursing. In the past few decades she had traveled extensively as a consultant for nursing organizations. In fact, while they lived in Iowa, she received a certificate for having logged more than two-million air miles. Now they were traveling again but this time for pleasure.

Saul and Mildred Gerson, like many others boarding the plane that day, were embarking on their first trip abroad. They had joined the Art Association because they had a special reason for going to Paris. Several years earlier, their son Bob had met a young Parisian named Micheline Tindel, a friend of his sister's, who helped him find an inexpensive hotel room during his first trip to Paris. When Bob phoned Micheline for help in communicating with the hotel manager in French, she invited him for dinner. Within the next few years, that meeting blossomed into a romance and they eventually became engaged. She had visited Atlanta and now she wanted her parents to meet the Gersons. The Art Association trip seemed like the perfect way for them to see Europe and spend time in Paris with Micheline and her parents.

It was also Rosalind Williams's first trip to Europe. Allene Goldsmith, who took her to the airport, remembers that everyone was having a wonderful time. At one point, Rosalind came up to her with an envelope saying that she was insured "up to the hilt." The two of them laughed. Since his whole family was traveling together, Fred Bull bought an insurance policy and named a close friend as beneficiary.

From the terminal, clusters of passengers wandered down the long corridor to the waiting room adjacent to Gate thirty-eight. Del Paige was telling everyone about the proposed Piedmont Park project; Winifred was at his side wearing a spray of orchids presented to her by the Art Association staff. Del was excited about plans for the cultural center that had just been announced in that day's Atlanta papers. Petitions showing support for the project were already in circulation, and Ivan and Louise Allen just happened to have copies on hand to pass around for people to sign.

The Paiges were traveling with their friends George and Sarah Beattie. He had recently retired from Wofford Oil, a subsidiary of Pure, having joined the company in 1919 and worked his way up to assistant manager. Sarah came from the small town of Dublin, Georgia, and in addition to raising their daughter, Sallie, and taking care of their East Pine Valley home, she volunteered for charities and participated in the garden club. Elsie and Charles Shaw were also in the waiting room. They had been married thirteen years earlier, both for the second time. Born in Philadelphia in 1900, Charles Shaw was a longtime employee of Sears Roebuck, who rose in the business to become superintendent for the organization's Atlanta mail order plant. No doubt they heard about the trip from another longtime Sears employee, Ruth McMillan.

Among the other couples waiting to board were Barron Glenn and his wife Grace. He was a manufacturer's agent dealing in electrical supplies and she was an amateur artist taking classes at the Atlanta Art Association. Homer Prater, one of the five unaccompanied men, was also in the electrical business. In his case it was Knapp Monarch Company that sold small appliances.

As most of the other single people traveling that day were women, this fifty-five year old bachelor—who lived with his mother in Atlanta but owned a vacation home on Sea Island— would be at no loss for companionship. One of those companions would probably be Virginia Wilson, a particularly good friend also taking the tour.

The travelers from Griffin—Dolly Brooks, along with Forest and Inez Cumming—were waiting near Gate thirty-eight. Forest Cumming was a former professor, having taught math at the University of Georgia from 1929 until 1952. After his retirement, Forest began practicing law in Griffin. His wife, Inez, a graduate of Shorter College, once taught in the public schools of Decatur and Quitman, Georgia, and for two years was manager of the University of Georgia Press. But her real love was art, and because she dabbled in painting, they had decided to sign up for the trip.

After standing around the waiting room in what seemed like an interminably long time, the crowd began its slow exit through Gate thirty-eight around one o'clock. Teresa Turner walked to the plane with her mother, Allee Tidmore, and her friend Mildred Dilts. Mary Elizabeth Schroder knew so many people going on the trip, especially her Sweetbriar roommate Henrietta Ayer, that she decided to come out to watch the takeoff.

There were hugs and kisses as the passengers walked out of the waiting room and strolled across the runway. In 1962 there was no such thing as security check points, so families and friends could follow the travelers outside and watch them climb aboard the plane. Onlookers took photographs while newsmen snapped shutters and aimed movie cameras. Reginald Poland, Director of the High Museum, was in the crowd standing outside on the runway. He walked with Paul Barnett onto the field, shaking hands with him and other passengers as they climbed the metal stairs. Vasser Woolley, with his hands on his hips and a camera dangling from his neck, stood by the jet watching people enter the aircraft.

Slowly they boarded the Air France chartered plane, labeled "Chateau d'Amboise." Most of the men wore sport coats, white shirts, ties, and hats; the women were dressed in comfortable traveling clothes, which in 1962 meant linen or cotton jackets over polyester or silk blouses, knee-length skirts, stockings, and high-heeled shoes. Many also wore trim pillboxes or straw hats and almost all had on corsages presented by well-wishers. And being Southern ladies, their hands were covered by white cotton gloves.

Susan Coltrane, dressed appropriately in a navy traveling suit, turned and waved as she boarded the jet. Once on the plane, she took her assigned seat next to Toni Wien and Frances Beers. The mood was jubilant as the passengers laughed about what they had done in preparation for the voyage, what they were taking, what they wished they had packed, and the trials and tribulations of stuffing so many items into undersized suitcases. Going abroad in 1962 had little of the humdrum monotony of today's routine overseas flights. Not only were the accommodations in coach class much roomier than they are today, but the travelers felt they were embarking on a unique adventure.

Smiling faces peered from the windows to wave once more at friends and relatives lining the sides of the runway; an excess amount of adrenaline flowed as they prepared for takeoff. At 1:45 P.M., the jet slowly pulled away from the gate. The crowd gathered next to the terminal waved handkerchiefs and banners as the airplane taxied down the runway, remaining there until they saw the "Chateau d'Amboise" lift its nose skyward and disappear.

On the one-and-a-half-hour flight between Atlanta and New York, each passenger was served a large lunch of ham, bologna, egg salad, turkey, roast beef, olives, pickles, fish salad and a fresh fruit—all washed down with champagne. The journey had truly begun in the luxurious manner promised. Clementina MacPherson and her two daughters sat up front in first class upon departure, but knew it was too good to last.

At 4:40 P.M., the plane landed at New York's Idlewild (now Kennedy) Airport, then one of the nation's only international departure points. Expecting to spend only a short time there for refueling, the Atlantans were dismayed when the pilot announced that their plane had mechanical trouble and the departure for France would be slightly delayed. Everyone piled into the terminal. After waiting for awhile, a few people decided to eat in the restaurant, but most had different ideas about how to tolerate the layover. Since they had been promised another gourmet meal en route to Paris, why spoil their appetites with an early dinner? Many ended up in the bar, where they engaged in their own "refueling" to celebrate the beginning of a long-awaited trip. The excitement level remained high as they sipped their cocktails and downed peanuts. But their "brief" stop stretched on for over four hours, too much booze was consumed, and creeping fatigue began to overtake them.

Finally the *Chateau d'Amboise* was repaired and ready to go. Once again the Atlantans filed aboard. By then it was after 9 P.M. When the plane was airborne, most of the women retreated to one of the lavatories to remove their hose, high heels, girdles, and traveling clothes, changing into "sleeping gear" for the overseas portion of the flight. After eating another elaborate meal, the excited group quieted down. As expected, the MacPherson family were ousted from their comfortable first-class seats and had to settle with sitting separately in coach for the seven-hour flight to Paris. Paul Barnett managed to catch one or two hours of sleep before the stewardesses woke everybody up for breakfast. After the delay in New York and reported mechanical trouble, Ruby Stow didn't sleep a wink. In a postcard mailed a few days after their arrival, she wrote to her sister-in-law in a shaky hand: "You keep praying I get home safely."

CHAPTER 9

❧ Trip to the Louvre

*D*uring the 1950s and early '60s, Paris was a mandatory stop on all tours of the Continent. The city, which had cast its spell over Americans from the days of Benjamin Franklin and Thomas Jefferson, had a special allure for the generation that lived through its occupation during World War II. For Americans—who grew teary when they heard the voices of Edith Piaf and Charles Trenet, sighed over Ernest Hemingway's *The Sun Also Rises,* or thrilled to *American in Paris* and *Moulin Rouge*—the banks of the Seine, the Rive Gauche, and Montmartre epitomized the romantic sublime.

The Atlantans arriving in Paris on May 10, 1962, expected to be smitten and they were. "The trip had a brilliant beginning," said Susan Coltrane Lowance. "As we entered Paris it was about eight o'clock in the morning, and it was brilliantly sunny. Even though it was early May, the window boxes in those wonderfully baroque European buildings were filled with flowers and it took your breath away. It was like no place we had ever seen before." That first view of Paris made the long journey and sleepless night worthwhile.

Horse chestnut trees and lilacs were also in full bloom and even Carroll Young, who hated to leave her Atlanta garden, seemed exuberant about the city's floral display. The only drawback was the weather. The thermometer registered fifty-five degrees, dropping below fifty degrees at night with periodic drizzle and rain. Having just come from the warm late spring of Atlanta, many complained about not having enough warm clothes. Paul Barnett, who had traveled several times to France, was knowledgeable enough to bring his winter suit, a scarf, and gloves. Most of the others, however, were freezing.

The majority of the group that arrived from Atlanta on May 10 spent the first night at the Hôtel du Louvre because the room was part of a package for both "Plan A," the $388 chartered plane fare, and "Plan B," the full tour. For those who weren't too jet-lagged, a visit to the Louvre—to fulfill the promise of the trip's title—was also part of the bargain. In 1962 the Baroque and Renaissance palace looked the same from the outside as it had when it served as a residence for Bourbon royalty. Baffled tourists had to wander through a labyrinth of hallways and galleries until they found the wide staircase topped by "Winged Victory," the famed relic of ancient Greece. Eventually they would find Leonardo's tiny *Mona Lisa,* if they could see it over the heads of the crowds gathered before it. Most Atlantans were following an American Express guide, who would lead them to that masterpiece and indicate a few others before hustling them back to the bus.

The hardiest of the Art Association tourists were also treated to a coach tour of the city at night and dinner at a "typical popular restaurant." On the following afternoon, those registered for "Plan

B" flew to London. The program seems to have been flexible enough for people to stay with the tour for a few days and then travel on their own. Several Atlantans, in fact, chose to stay in Paris for a few extra days at the beginning of the trip. Clementina MacPherson and her daughters, Lee Virgin and Frances Hill, had rooms at the St. James & D'Albany. Not deterred by the dismal weather, they toured all the requisite sights, from a stop at Napoleon's tomb to an excursion to Versailles. In the evenings, Lee and Frances often left their mother at the hotel and went off on their own, one night attending the Follies Bergère and another watching Parisians dance the Twist at a nightclub. All three saw a performance of *Carmen* at the Paris Opera, and Lee teased Frances about speaking French "with mouth and both hands."

The Youngs and Laniers also remained in Paris a few extra days. Sykes Young told his daughter that "gay Paree" seemed to be everything they expected. One favorite spot on the Americans' "must do" list was lunch on the second tier of the Eiffel Tower, and the two couples made that stop. "All the men and boys have long hair," Carroll wrote, "at least Sykes and I think they should have a hair cut." It was comforting to unexpectedly run into friends from home, especially Jim and Josephine Robertson, who happened to be in Paris when the tour arrived and joined several of them for dinner or cocktails.

Jet travel was still so new in 1962 that most Americans had not yet broken with the old notion of the "grand tour." A mandatory checklist of every major city, along with the smaller "interesting" bastions of culture, was a necessity for all those aspiring to present themselves as sophisticated and worldly. If Americans of past centuries were able to accomplish these stops over a period of months or even years, those of the mid-twentieth century could "do it all" sufficiently in three weeks.

The escorted tourists, who flew from Paris to London on May 11, found themselves inundated with "obligatory" sights. Each day, approximately forty-five Atlantans would board busses early in the morning, take a half-day excursion, stop for lunch, and then embark on an afternoon tour. On the day after their arrival in London, for example, they were whisked away from the Waldorf Hotel to have a fast-paced look at Trafalgar Square, the Law Courts, Fleet Street, London Bridge, St. Paul's Cathedral, and the Bank of England, with a visit to the Tower of London to view the crown jewels. Because the weather in London was even worse than in Paris, they waited in the long "queue" at the Tower under umbrellas. Then they had a brief shopping detour at the Old Curiosity Shop, a tourist-oriented restoration of the store made famous by Charles Dickens. In the afternoon, they drove past Albert Hall, Marble Arch, Hyde Park Corner, Ten Downing Street, and the Parliament Buildings and stopped for a visit to Westminster Abby. "We have been sightseeing all day," Ruby Stowe wrote on the evening after the marathon run through London. "Boy! I mean it's bitter cold here. Wish I had brought a heavier coat." She had little time to rest or warm up because the next day they again boarded the busses, this time heading to Oxford in the morning with lunch in an old English inn before traveling up to Stratford-on-Avon to see the "Shakespeare Country."

Del Paige took on the mantle of tour leader. Margaret Turner called Del and Winifred "the mama and papa of the tour group." As president of the Art Association, he assumed the role that he had so often taken in his years of community service. And because of his commitment to the Forward Atlanta campaign, he wanted to make certain that the Atlantans exhibited a proper decorum. He even carried a little book with instructions for correctly pronouncing the names of famous artists, which became a joke with the group because Paige seemed to think that information was necessary to keep his flock from committing a *faux pas*. Only a few years earlier, *The Ugly American* by William J. Lederer and Eugene Burdick had denounced tourists from the United States, who treated foreigners condescendingly and generally made nuisances of themselves. The entire Atlanta group—conscious of this negative image—tried diligently to exhibit its best and most inconspicuous Southern manners.

On Monday, May 14, the Atlantans were awarded a much needed "day at leisure" in London. Some no doubt bought tickets for either a matinee or evening performance at a West End theater, while other members of the group attended a cocktail party at the Grosvenor House, hosted by the Vol T. Blacknalls of Atlanta, who had been visiting in London for several weeks. The Laniers and Youngs caught up with the group in London that day. Carroll Young was enamored with the city, especially the flowers. "All stores, banks, post offices have window boxes filled with primroses, English daisies, lilacs, tulips," she wrote, and they are "in bloom everywhere." Sykes Young was so captivated by London that he wanted to come back for a much longer trip and bring their daughter and her sons.

Before leaving home, Susan Coltrane had promised to have dinner with Kathleen (Mrs. Mason) Lowance from Atlanta. Traveling with her friend, Claire (Mrs. Hixon) Kinsella, she had been touring the world since February. Along the way they had been joined by several Atlantans—including Mrs. Kinsella's husband—and they all converged on the British capital where they planned to meet for dinner at Quaglino's. When she arrived at the St. James restaurant, Susan was surprised to discover that Kathleen's son, Mason Lowance Jr., a graduate student at Oxford was included in the party. They had known each other as children growing up in Atlanta, but had not been reacquainted as adults. They were the youngest people at the table and sat together, discovering many common interests during a long conversation. When the evening ended, they promised to keep in touch, and Susan gave Mason a copy of her itinerary for the rest of her European journey.

On the next day, May 15, the escorted tour took a morning plane to Amsterdam. By all counts, the spirits of the tourists had not been dampened by the cool, wet weather. American Express had arranged fewer organized tours in the Dutch city, which probably pleased those who wanted to wander around looking at the steep houses lining canals and see Rembrandt's master-pieces in the Rijksmuseum. The following afternoon, the tour again boarded a bus to drive out to Volendam, a small fishing village where the residents still wore the traditional costumes. Several of those residents—tall Dutch women in starched white caps, aprons, and wooden shoes—posed with several of the Atlantans in dripping rain coats and plastic hoods. In the rain, they boarded a launch to visit the Isle of Marken, another quaint village favored by tourists; and on the way back to Amsterdam, they stopped at a farm to sample Dutch cheese.

All along the way, they gathered gifts and mementos. In the years when Americans went abroad clutching *Europe on $5 a Day,* the average tourist could make it to the compulsory sights, eat well, sleep comfortably, and shop extensively for a relatively reasonable price. American Express had booked moderate first-class hotels for the Atlantans and based their tour rate on double occupancy. Those women not traveling with a spouse, family member, or close friend were assigned roommates, many of whom were total strangers. Susan Coltrane roomed with Puddin' Humphrey, whom she only knew casually before the tour started, but by the time they parted, the two Agnes Scott graduates had become good friends.

When dinners were not included in the package, the Atlantans usually paired off with old or new friends. Susan Coltrane, then in her mid-twenties, was touched that people twice her age always included her in their dinner plans. "I think tours some time can break off into little cliques," she mused, "and I have no sense that happened on this trip." The food was also relatively reasonable—the only setback was having to constantly deal with different foreign currencies.

After spending two days in Amsterdam, the group flew to Zurich and boarded motor coaches headed for Lucerne. That small lakeside city snuggled in the shadow of the Alps was a favorite destination of Americans. In addition to its plethora of Swiss watches, cuckoo clocks, and chocolates, the town's greatest attraction was the "Lion of Lucerne," a large sculpted beast carved into a rock. The nearby Alps drew crowds to its summits. The Atlantans ascended Mount Pilatus on a cog wheel train after crossing Lake Lucerne on a steamer, returning either by train or cable car to the town of Kriens at the mountain's base.

They didn't need to go to the top of a mountain to find winter. It was actually snowing the day they left Lucerne. "So far," Margaret Turner reported from Rome, "our summer clothes have remained packed in our suitcases. We have not been out of our winter coats a single day since leaving Atlanta May 9."

On the morning of May 21, the group left Switzerland on a passenger train headed across the Alps to Venice. When they settled into the Hotel Luna, they found that Lee Virgin, Clementina MacPherson, and Frances Hill were there at another hotel. The Youngs and Laniers, who had gone from London to Vienna, were also in Venice staying at the Hotel Danieli on the Grand Canal. The weather was not much better in Italy than it had been in northern Europe, so the planned walks around the bridges and canals to the Doges Palace and St. Mark's were wet and bone-chilling. Everyone made the obligatory stop at St. Mark's Square and posed for snapshots opposite the huge Byzantine cathedral with pigeons perched on their arms and shoulders.

The chilly dampness that had plagued them since the beginning of the trip finally invaded their bodies in Venice, as one by one the Atlantans came down with what was reported as a respiratory virus, but was more likely a type of flu. Margaret Turner reported: "Some say the virus was caused by exposure. But we can't decide if we had been exposed to too many paintings and nude sculpture, too many dark and dank castles, too many steps, too much rain, or too much of each other." Some said that the water might have "downed" them. "And while wine is consumed by some as a water substitute," Margaret continued, "many unwary souls drink water anywhere and everywhere without any difficulties." Ruby Stow still dropped her "purifying pill" in each glass before drinking it, but others "found that a dash of Scotch or Bourbon makes the best water purifier in the world."

The illness apparently didn't slow the pace. On Tuesday, May 22, they boarded motor coaches for the long ride to Florence, with many members of the group suffering from high fever, a cough, and laryngitis. A Florentine doctor recommended by the American Embassy came to their rooms at the Hotel Baglioni to dispense sulfa pills and administer penicillin shots, which helped get most of them back on their feet. Those feeling well enough toured the Uffizi Gallery, the Pitti Palace, the Duomo, the Medici Chapel, and all the other landmarks of this gem-like Renaissance city. On Thursday, Allee Tidmore and Mildred Dilts visited the studio of an artist named Lido Bagni, whom they had arranged to meet. Bagni picked up the two women at their hotel, gave them a tour of his studio, and took them to lunch (or more likely the women treated the artist to lunch). A few years earlier, Allee had sent photographs of her children and instructed the Florentine to paint portraits, which he subsequently completed and shipped to Atlanta.

By the time their motor coach approached Rome on May 25, the weather had improved tremendously, and the party of Atlantans resumed its old vivacity and high spirits. For many, their four days in the Eternal City were the best of all. They toured the essential sights—from the Vatican, St. Peters, and the Sistine Chapel to the Forum, Coliseum, and other monuments built by the ancient Romans. After two full days of sightseeing, they had two days of leisure, which most spent acquiring antiques, leather goods, souvenirs, and works of art. Friends living in Rome took Margaret Turner and Raiford Ragsdale to the trendy nightclub, Bricktop, a hangout for such celebrities as Elizabeth Taylor, Richard Burton, and Charlton Heston. The flamboyant redhead owner of the club was out of the city, so the ladies from Atlanta had to settle for her sister, Elsa.

News from home reached the Art Association tourists as they traversed Europe. Some of it—including word that the Piedmont Park project had been placed on the upcoming bond referendum—was welcome news. But a stock market crash on May 29 cast a gloomy pall over the tour. The Atlantans were having breakfast at the Hotel de la Ville in Rome when they read the shocking news in the *Herald-Tribune*—the Dow Jones average had dropped 5.71%, which was a significant loss in the financial markets of the early '60s. Nine million shares had been traded, an amount comparable to several billion shares today. The losses of Roby Robinson, Del Paige, and several major stockholders in Coca-Cola were devastating. Although the newspaper warned Americans not to panic, the group from Atlanta was shattered by the news and anxious to return home and set their finances in order.

On the day of the stock market disaster, Susan Coltrane bid the group farewell. All along she had been planning to stay several additional weeks to see more of Italy, tour Austria, and visit her former roommate from Agnes Scott, Katy Blondeau, who lived in Paris. As she prepared to leave, everyone hovered around, warning her to be careful and promising that as soon as they returned to Atlanta they would call her mother to report that Susan was doing just fine. She assured her companions that she would look for items they had been trying to find, in particular a utensil for shaving butter. Before going to Austria, Susan traveled by train to Naples and then returned to Florence because she had been too ill to see it on the initial stop.

The Youngs and the Laniers were also touring Italy. When they flew into Rome from Venice, Nell Lanier's sister-in-law, Barron Hunnicutt, picked them up at the airport and drove them around Rome. With Barron at the wheel, they headed north, visiting Siena, Florence, and Assisi. In Caronna, they had lunch with Sykes Young's associate in the marble business, and from there they drove to Portofino near Genoa, the port near Bill Hunnicutt's anchored ship. Nell Lanier described Portofino as "a combination of Jupiter [Florida] and Highlands [North Carolina]." Their stay there provided their first chance to rest after what Nell described as "three weeks with sore feet and tired legs." She admitted, however, that much to her "surprise and delight," she was "not near ready to return" home. In Portofino, they celebrated Tommy's fiftieth birthday at a dinner with the Hunnicutts overlooking the Mediterranean. Nell gave her husband a pitcher she had purchased in Florence and the seaside celebration turned out to be a roaring success.

While the escorted tour was wending its way from England to Italy, those who opted to travel independently were traveling elsewhere in Europe. Vasser Woolley had spent three happy weeks with Mildred and Max Seydel in Belgium. During the visit, he and his sister reestablished the close relationship they had enjoyed before his marriage, and they made tentative arrangements to spend the winter together at Wooley's Atlanta house. One evening Vasser, Mildred, and Max met the Atlanta group for dinner in Amsterdam and did some additional touring of the area. Meanwhile, Mildred Seydel's ex-daughter-in-law, Helen, was relaxing in Florence, contemplating the idea of spending more time there in the near future.

Paul Barnett was thoroughly enjoying Paris. From his comfortable four dollar-per-day room at the Hôtel de France & Choiseul, he explored all corners of the city, finding stained glass windows in a number of surprising places. During his excursions, he would stop at street corners to make notes or sketches, leaning against automobiles to jot things down or ducking into doorways to escape the constant rain. "Boy this book is going to be a dilly," he wrote his wife. "I am more and more enthused." Part of this enthusiasm was for the people. "I have watched them above ground and under ground," he remarked, "in the parks and along the streets . . . It is a surging life here."

On a few occasions, Barnett took day trips to surrounding towns, especially Bourges, where he found the glass to be "magnificent." Occasionally he would attend a Bach recital or a Mozart Mass at Notre Dame. On most nights, however, he was happy to dine in small inexpensive restaurants, like the one near the Palais Royal, paying anywhere from $1.20 to $1.60 for dinner with an extra 30¢ for a half-bottle of wine or 17¢ for a glass. The food, the wine, and walks around the city were good for him, and he told his wife he was feeling better than he had in months.

While most of the Atlanta tourists were wet and cold, the Crimms and the Patzs were basking in the Mediterranean sunshine. They flew from Paris to Cyprus, before moving on to Cairo, which as expected they found "filthy" but "well worth the trip." Jan Crimm wrote her children that their "geography and social study [sic] books describe this important Nile Valley perfectly" with its pyramids and "entirely different" ways of living. That, she added "is what makes life and travel interesting." From Egypt the two couples flew to Tel Aviv. During their four day stay, they traversed the entire country, which then included neither the Gaza Strip nor West Bank. But even though the distances from top to bottom were then relatively short, they clocked over 750 miles in "easy stages." In Beersheba at the edge of Negev Dessert, they encountered 110 degree heat, and in Carmel they discovered that the Israelis made wine, which they sold all over the world. From Israel, they flew to Istanbul, which they found "beautiful and relaxing" and ended their odyssey in Athens before returning to Paris.

Not far away, Bill and Helen Cartledge were also enjoying the warm Mediterranean climate in Athens and on the Greek isles. Frances Beers was also in Greece, writing her friend Doris Lockerman that the experience "exceeds anything I could have ever dreamed. These islands are so enthralling, erupting as they do so dramatically from the incandescent sea. No wonder Homer was inspired to write *The Illiad* and *The Odyssey.* " Morgan and Ted Cantey had spent a week in Italy before going to Spain. After touring the country, they went to Madrid to visit Morgan's brother-in-law, Ivy W. Duggan, an attaché at the United States Embassy. The Canteys were daunted to find "so many cathedrals of unbelievable grandeur often in the midst of the most abject and depressing poverty." Tom and Charlotte Little were collecting evidence of seventeenth century life in Northern Europe; Katharine Bleckley and Margaret Nutting were visiting old friends in Britain, while the Youngs and Laniers were ending their jaunt by spending a few days in Switzerland. Puddin' Humphreys left the tour to join her sister-in-law, Elizabeth Bealer, in Germany. While visiting an Augsburg museum, she was thrilled to discover her own paintings of a Mississippi steamboat that she had once given to German friends.

On Wednesday, May 30, the escorted tour flew back into Paris for a four day stay. Milton Bevington was waiting there at Orly, having come from Atlanta to surprise his wife, Betsy, and her mother, Dell Rickey. He was planning to greet them when they returned on the scheduled flight from Rome. But much to his amazement, they did not descend the stairs with the rest of the group. When he questioned some of the Atlantans, he found that Betsy and her mother opted to delay their arrival and spend a few more hours nosing around Rome. Milton, therefore, went ahead to the Relais Bisson—a tiny 400-year-old hotel on the left bank overlooking the Seine—where the two women were scheduled to stay. Finally late that afternoon, Betsy and Dell checked in and were shocked and delighted to find Milton awaiting them. Their delayed arrival, however, was soon forgotten as they set about to enjoy a slightly warmer and decidedly dryer Paris than they had left two-and-a-half weeks earlier.

In order to enjoy the good weather, Milton later remembered, workers all over Paris decided to walk off the job. Accustomed to encountering unannounced strikes, Parisians had learned to take museum closings and transportation delays in stride. A national holiday, followed by a religious holiday, caused additional inconveniences that further shut down the French capital. But that scarcely deterred the Atlantans. "In Paris everyone was doing what they wanted to do," Milton recalled. "People on the trip had gotten to know each other, so we'd walk around the town and you'd run into people, you'd meet lots of people.

Everybody was having a great time." Like Milton, Randy Berry showed up in Paris after his business trip and planned to fly home with his wife, Anne, and her sister-in-law, Lydia Black.

Mildred Gerson was thoroughly enjoying Paris. She and Saul had returned there after visiting Switzerland and Italy, probably traveling at times with the escorted tour. Once again their daughter-in-law-to-be took them around the city. Mildred loved antiques, and Micheline introduced her to everything from flea markets to quaint little out-of-the way shops. Micheline remembered bumping into others from the trip engaging in a similar folly. It was a "beautiful trip," Micheline mused. "People would meet in restaurants and talk. Paris was not the same then, it was a smaller city. They had the best of the best and I think they had become friends."

Those on the escorted tour, not worn out by sightseeing, once more boarded the busses to see both modern and historical Paris, with another short visit to the Louvre. On Friday, June 1, they went to Versailles. Micheline, who went with her future in-laws, remembered one funny incident. As they drew closer to the palace, Mildred Gerson was so taken by everything she had read and heard about the palace that she was certain she would be transported back into history and see kings and queens. Just as she said that, they encountered a crew of actors wearing wigs and eighteenth-century costumes, wandering out of the former Bourbon residence after shooting a scene from *Angelique and the King*. Mildred stopped in her tracks. "Pinch me," she gasped. "I don't know if it's the wine, but I think I see people coming out of the castle dressed as they were then." Micheline actually had to steady her, because the shock of seeing those people caused her to shake.

When they finished touring Versailles, many of the Atlantans lined up in the courtyard to pose for a photographer. Raiford

Ragsdale knew the value of publicity and sent the photograph to her daughter as a postcard. On the back was the list of names— Raiford, Pierce and Adelaide McDonald, Ruth McMillan, Pat and Chris Allen, Beaty Henson, Alee Tidmore, Mildred Dilts, Lillie Minier, Theodosia Barnett, Margheretta Luty, Winifred and Del Paige, Virginia Cowan, George and Sarah Beattie, Ruby Stow, Charles Shaw, Mary and Harry Boon, and Saul Gerson.

In their spare time, everyone shopped. Many had the names of couturiers or perfumeries that catered to Americans. In 1962, U. S. customs allowed citizens to bring only $100 worth of goods per person back into the country. With the relatively inexpensive price of goods in Europe, travelers figured out ways to circumvent these restrictions by mailing their purchases home. However, another restriction was the limit on the dollar value that could be mailed to one person per day. With the help of the merchants, American tourists sent several packages to different people, marked with low estimates of the contents.

Other Atlantans spent time in Paris seeing friends and family. Henrietta Ayer visited with her daughter, Penny Armstrong, who was attending the Sorbonne as part of the Hollins College Abroad program. She had begun her classes in Paris a few months earlier, during the final semester of her sophomore year, and had not seen her mother since leaving Atlanta a few months earlier.

David Cogland returned to Paris after visiting his uncle in Germany and traveling in Europe with Tito Hidealdo, a colleague from art school. He was excited about the contacts he had made with French art dealers and was delighted to learn that his friend, Doug Davis, would be returning on the charter flight to Atlanta in a seat that Hidealdo had originally booked for himself. Then at the last minute, Hidealdo decided to visit his family in the Philippines, and Davis took the seat so he could return and help his mother decorate her new house in East Point. His father was one of aviation's early stunt pilots and had operated a daily air passenger service between Atlanta and Birmingham. In 1935—while leading a trophy race in Ohio—his plane went down in a fiery crash, killing him. This accident marked yet another ironic link between those aboard the Air France charter and fatal airline disasters.

Doug Davis moved to Paris in 1958, and, during that time, had become recognized in the city as an up and coming artist. He first discovered Europe while serving for two years as a soldier in Germany, and during his tour of duty, he painted a mural in the enlisted men's club in Frankfurt. After returning home, Doug attended the Atlanta Art Institute and painted several murals in both Atlanta and Miami. Encouraged by these successes, he left home to study art at the Sorbonne and Grand Chaumier Academy in Paris. He remained there to paint portraits of celebrities, and among his clients were Vivien Leigh, Rex Harrison, Rise Stevens, and Edith Piaf.

The Atlantans' return visit to Paris was a tremendous success from all accounts. "I'm stuffed with sights as well as food," wrote Rosalind Williams; and Raiford Ragsdale told her daughter: "We've had 4 wonderful clear but cold days which, as you know, are not enough. So many beautiful places, and things to buy." But after three weeks away, the Atlantans were ready to return home. "As the time grows near," Paul Barnett wrote his wife, "I can hardly wait to see you." Although he admitted he was not looking forward to the ninety-two degree weather, he concluded: "I will soon be counting the hours."

CHAPTER 10

⚌ Orly Airport

*I*n 1962, Paris's only international airport was very informal compared to its later incarnation as an efficient but sterile jumble of security gates and long passageways. A cheerful reunion took place there on June 3. Waiting to leave, the Atlantans on the escorted tour were greeting the fellow passengers who had traveled on their own. Everyone's mood was joyous. Several of the women were comparing purchases: Florentine pottery and leather, French scarves, Dutch chocolates. New friends and old were savoring the last minutes of being in Europe.

Milton Bevington accompanied his wife and mother-in-law to Orly that day. He and Betsy never flew together—a safety precaution protecting their three young sons. Scheduled to take a later Pan Am flight to New York, he would make connections and rejoin his family that evening in Atlanta. In the waiting room, Dell Rickey begged her son-in-law to take her seat aboard the charter and she would return on the later flight. Milton and Betsy considered it for a minute, but decided to stick with their rule of never flying together.

Paul Dossans was circulating among the passengers, answering questions and making certain all documents were in order. As the district manager for Air France in Atlanta, he had flown to Paris four days earlier to supervise the return flight. Around noon, he checked to be sure he could account for everyone. But a head-count came up short. The temptation to buy more gloves, perfume, leather goods, whiskey, and last-minute souvenirs in the duty-free shops had enticed a few people to pick up last minute items before returning home. Dossans was getting nervous. The flight was already late for departure and they had a schedule to meet. Finally around 12:15 P.M., the last shoppers breathlessly appeared and the group began to board.

Micheline and her parents walked arm-in-arm out to the plane with Saul and Mildred Gerson. When they reached the edge of the runway, the two couples embraced, happily anticipating future get-togethers after their children were married. Micheline remembered that Mildred was wearing a pink hat when she turned and waved vigorously at the top of the stairs. Then she and her husband disappeared along with the others into the waiting Air France jet, labeled *Chateau de Sully.*

Aboard the jet, the passengers settled into their seats, 20 people in first-class, 102 in coach. They were greeted by Françoise Authie, Jacqueline Gillet, and Marcel Lugon, assigned to serve economy class while Genevieve Barot tended the twenty passengers seated in first-class. As usual, the flight attendants closed the door and walked around the cabin, distributing newspapers and candy. It was such "a happy group" of passengers, one of the stewardesses commented. Having flown numerous charter flights, she was accustomed to all manner of American tourists. But these were "better educated and courteous," she observed.

Captain Roland Hoche, a thirty-nine-year-old pilot with over 14,000 hours flying time, welcomed them aboard the *Chateau de Sully,* a Boeing 707 reserved exclusively for charter service. The two-year-old aircraft had logged 4,491 flight hours, most of them transporting French and American tourists across the Atlantic. Just the previous May, it had been thoroughly examined by Air France and found to have no mechanical problems of any kind. As usual, the plane was scheduled to make the 3,289 mile trip across the ocean in seven hours and twenty-eight minutes and would stop in New York for refueling. The passengers would go through customs before the plane flew to Atlanta with its final stop in Houston.

At 12:25, the captain advised the crew to prepare for takeoff. They were already late because of the last-minute shoppers. After ascertaining that all passengers were comfortable and properly belted, the three flight attendants in coach retreated to the rear of the plane and strapped themselves into two collapsible benches. Minutes later, the blue and silver jet taxied down Runway 26. The green light flashed in the control tower indicating takeoff. Captain Hoche accelerated the engines, expecting to propel the nose upward and lift off of the ground. Then he noticed something wrong, a signal flashed indicating that the tail stabilizers were not operating properly. The pilot had to act fast. Even though he had passed the "point of no return," he tried frantically to stop. But it was too late.

Watching the plane taxi, someone in the Orly control tower pushed an alarm button. Clearly the plane should have lifted off of the ground by now. Later investigators concluded that when

Hoche reversed the engines, the jet had already reached 160-180 knots. Thus when he slammed on the brakes, all eight tires burned out causing the craft to veer to one side still moving at a very fast speed. Inside the cabin, the passengers heard an unexpected reduction of engine noise as Captain Hoche attempted to decelerate by throwing the engines into reverse. Then they lost consciousness with the impact of the rapid deceleration.

At the end of Runway 26, a hill sloped down and then rose sharply. When the aircraft plunged into the gully, it was still intact, but the attempt to decelerate caused it to list to the right, slam through an airport fence, and crash into a row of concrete posts topped by approach-lights. These poles punctured the wings, tore open the fuel cells, and with the plane still moving at full speed, the engines fell off, the tail blew away, and the airplane clipped nearby houses before ending its drunken gyrations in the middle of a field. The fuel ignited and flames ripped through the fuselage, engulfing the entire craft. Only a minute or two elapsed between Hoche's last maneuver and the fatal fire. The sudden change in pressure and simultaneous explosion blessedly killed those in the cabin instantly. They never heard the explosion, nor inhaled the smoke, nor felt the fire.

Residents of Villeneuve-le-Roi, the village that bordered the airfield, were having leisurely Sunday luncheons on that sunny June day. Some had just returned from the annual parade to commemorate the liberation of French prisoners of war in June 1944. Other townspeople were picnicking in nearby meadows. Accustomed to jets roaring overhead, they paid little attention to noise. But this one was distinctively different. The rolling boom followed by black smoke meant trouble. Men, women, and children rushed out of their houses, some with napkins still tied around their necks. Firemen wearing uniforms from the liberation parade also came running and attempted to pour water and foam on the roaring fire. Meanwhile Sunday drivers on their way to the country picked up news of the crash on their car radios and diverted their excursions to converge on the crash scene. The police were moving rapidly to cordon off the area, but they were having problems keeping onlookers away.

Smoldering wreckage and debris were scattered everywhere. Nearby houses were damaged, some severely. Around the ground lay strewn pieces of the aircraft mixed with opened suitcases, items of clothing, and assorted other belongings of the passengers. "I saw the flames billow into the air," said Mme. Anna Lyer who lived across the street and downhill from where the fuselage landed. "There was so much fire and no one dared to go near." A neighbor, Mme. Robert Metternich, said that the fire "flew up the sides" of her house. She ran out of the back door but had to retreat to avoid the shooting flames. Her legs were slightly singed from that experience. The house adjacent to hers was gutted when the flaming jet engine ripped through it, but luckily, nobody was inside. An off-duty gendarme also had his legs burned as he vainly attempted a rescue operation. Then the ambulances arrived expecting to assist in rescuing passengers. But all they could pull from the wreckage was a tangle of charred bodies, still strapped into their seats.

Milton Bevington watched the plane taxi down the runway, move past the terminal, disappear from view, and then reappear in the distance. It seemed to be taking a long time to get off the ground. He saw it climb briefly, bump down again, rise up briefly, and then bounce on the runway, its tires emitting a puff of white smoke upon contact. Then he watched the plane plow through the fence as plumes of black smoke darkened the horizon. He realized there had been an accident, but there was no indication of its severity.

He stumbled out of the observation area, still unsure about

what had transpired. Time and sequences of events tend to merge and distort in moments of extreme shock, leaving Bevington remembering a series of jarring vignettes. He recalls meeting a man named John Schneider, the Southeastern director for Air France stationed in Atlanta, who just happened to be at Orly en route to a vacation in Greece. When Schneider found out about the crash, he quickly changed his plans and went to help handle the emergency. After escorting Bevington down into another waiting room, Schneider went out to view the crash scene and returned with the unwelcome news that the wreck was "pretty bad." Then the two men went over to a temporary Air France operations area where airline officials were checking off lists of people aboard the plane.

In that room, Bevington remembered seeing two young women. Both were cut and bruised and sobbing uncontrollably. He was told that they were Air France stewardesses from the *Chateau de Sully*. One of them, Françoise Authie, later spoke to reporters in a nearby military hospital where she was being treated for burns received during the accident. Choked with emotion, Authie said that she remembered a series of bumps as the airplane racked from side to side. "Everything happened so fast," she said. "There were these jolts, and all the dishes in the cupboard broke." Suddenly she heard a deafening noise, after which she lost consciousness. The next thing she remembered was finding herself in the grass, the seat belt still strapped around her and wrecked bits of the fuselage all about. "Then I heard Jacqueline calling me," she related.

The two airline hostesses looked over at the black smoke pouring from the plane and realized there was no way they could help. "We were completely shocked," Françoise told reporters, "and we began running away, helping each other as we went." One of her shoes was trapped under some of the debris. Rather than try to retrieve it, she kicked off the other shoe and ran in her stocking feet. "We came to a fence," she said, "and climbed it like monkeys. It must have been there that I cut my feet and hands." Then they spotted a farmhouse across the field. People standing in the yard were waving, so they ran toward the house as fast as they could. When they encountered a second fence, someone was there with a ladder to make their climb easier.

After the women reached the farmhouse, they were transported by authorities to the terminal. Bevington stood nearby as investigators questioned them. It was the description given by the two bruised, burned, and sobbing women—the only ones able to walk away from the crash—that made Bevington chillingly aware that everyone else on the plane was dead. Still in a daze, he told Schneider and others that he had to make a Pan Am flight to New York at five o'clock. He was anxious to return to Atlanta to be with his three boys. Not just now, he was told. As a witness to the disaster, he would have to be questioned by the FBI and French authorities.

After the Gersons boarded the plane, Micheline Tindel and her parents decided to have lunch in the restaurant on an upper tier of the Orly terminal. From there they could watch the planes depart. As they waited to be served, they thought they saw a puff of smoke on the horizon. A few minutes later fire engines and ambulances were rushing across the field. No one seemed to know what had happened. It looked like there might be a fire, but they were not unduly alarmed. M. Tindel told his wife and daughter that he was certain it was only a minor incident, but at their prompting he agreed to go downstairs and find out what had happened. He returned a while later, grim-faced. The smoke was indeed coming from the Air France charter, he reported, and suggested that they go out to the scene of the accident to inquire about possible assistance. Micheline remembers that her mother said, "We can take the two of them [the Gersons] to our apartment and get a nurse if they need it. And then they can go home." "It never occurred to us," said Micheline, "that anybody was dead."

In a few minutes, Micheline and her parents were on the edge of the crash scene. Black smoke continued to billow out of the wreckage. In a vain attempt to quench it, firemen sprayed water and foam. M. Tindel had a press pass, so he was able to walk over to converse with one of the gendarmes and returned to tell his wife and daughter the dreadful news. Realizing there was nothing they could do to help the crash victims, the Tindel family made a rapid retreat.

Meanwhile rescue workers searched for survivors. They found only one, the steward Michel Lugan. Like Authie and Gillet, he had been blown from the tail of the jet when it exploded. Rushed to a nearby hospital, he lingered for awhile but eventually died. When the official death list was finally released, it contained the names of 130 people: 106 from Atlanta, 16 from other parts of the United States, and 8 crew members.

When they returned home, M. Tindel gave his daughter a tall glass of Scotch. It was a strong drink "like I never had in my life," Micheline recalled. "And he said you have to compose yourself. The funny thing," she said, "is that I was speaking English, I was not speaking French." Unaware of the language shift, she had to be reminded of it later by her mother. When she finished her drink and garnered the strength, she picked up the phone to call Bob in Atlanta. From the way he answered the phone, Micheline realized that he already knew.

Penny Armstrong was in her room shortly after noon that Sunday, studying for her Sorbonne exams, with the radio playing softly in the background. On the previous evening she left her books long enough to have dinner with her mother, Henrietta Ayer, and her traveling companion, Sally Benson. They had talked excitedly about the European tour that Henrietta and Sally had just completed, and Penny told them about her experiences as a student in Paris. She had a surprise for her mother, a charcoal drawing of herself done on a Montmartre street near her apartment. Henrietta tucked it in her bag, kissed her daughter goodbye, and told Penny to have a wonderful summer. She'd see her in the fall.

As she studied on that Sunday afternoon, Penny's mind kept wandering. It was hard to focus on her books on such a beautiful early summer day. Suddenly, an agitated commentary interrupted the peaceful music. Something was definitely happening, but assuming it was a domestic problem and not wanting to bother translating the French, she ignored it. In an hour or so, her concentration was again broken, this time by the telephone. It was her step-father, Dr. Darrell Ayer, calling from Atlanta. There had been an accident at Orly, he said, and he had arranged a flight for her to come home the following day. As she hung up the phone in her numbed state, Penny realized what the hysterical French broadcaster must have been talking about.

On that same bright, sunny afternoon, Peggy and Dick Schiffman were greeted by a clerk holding up a newspaper as they walked into their Paris hotel. They had arrived from Atlanta the previous evening and started their vacation with a day-trip to Versailles. Returning to the hotel, they gazed at the newspaper, not fully comprehending the French. Therefore, the clerk dashed out and returned with a special edition of the *Herald Tribune*. Shocked by what they read, they went up to their room "and just sort of sat there." Finally Dick decided to call the American Embassy and say they were from Atlanta, had friends on the plane, and were offering their help. The embassy official—who had apparently received many such calls—told them to check back in a couple of days, because there would probably be a memorial service. Since there was nothing they could do to help, the Schiffmans carried on with their plans to see Paris for the first time. But we felt "so undermined," Peggy said. "Everywhere we went touched a nerve," because upon discovering they were from Atlanta, total strangers would offer their condolences.

Bevington ended up spending a very painful and unexpected night in a Paris hotel. After talking to FBI agents for several hours, he was becoming increasingly worried about his three sons staying in Atlanta with a sitter. Several frustrating attempts to make long-distance calls finally put him in touch with a friend, who promised to take the boys to his vacation house in North Georgia. That way, Bevington figured, they would not learn about the deaths of their mother and grandmother from television or radio, and he would be able to tell them when he returned.

On that same Sunday night, Susan Coltrane arrived in Innsbruck, Austria. When she checked into her hotel, the clerk said her mother in Atlanta had been trying to reach her, so Susan called home. In stunned disbelief, she learned that the people with whom she had been traveling for the past three weeks had gone down in fiery flames. Alone and grieving, Susan was uncertain what to do next. During their phone conversation, Elizabeth Coltrane begged her daughter not to return to Atlanta. It would be too hard to face a city in deep mourning. Following her mother's advice, she prepared to continue on her pre-planned itinerary. Little did she then know that by spending the next few months in Europe, her life would change forever.

CHAPTER 11

❧ The Day Atlanta Stood Still

*I*t was barely dawn on June 3 when Linda Williams woke up terrified. She and her husband had taken their two small sons to the family lake house near Anniston, Alabama. Jumping out of bed, fearing something had happened to the boys, she dashed into their bedroom. Two-year-old Chris was nowhere to be found. "I looked frantically all over the cabin," she remembered. "We always kept the outside doors locked. I pulled at the back door which opened easily and ran down the steep steps." Hastening toward the lake, Linda spotted a tiny figure in the emerging daylight. It was "Chris standing quietly at the end of the long dock." She edged up slowly. "I'll always remember my fear as I tried not to startle him." It was 6:30 A.M. Her mother Rosalind was due at the Atlanta airport later that day.

At that same moment in Columbus, Georgia, Ann Boon Rhea

woke up with a start. She had just had a vivid dream about her parents, Harry and Mary Boon. It was an "exact picture" of them both, "not in distress, not wildly happy, just ordinary looks," she recalled. Before going back to sleep, she rolled over and looked at the clock and noticed it was 6:30 A.M. A few hours later, she was fixing breakfast for her three small children when the phone rang. Ann remembers that a friend asked "sort of strangely" what they were doing that day. She replied that she was going to a christening and then driving up to Atlanta to meet her parents at the airport. There was a pause before the friend asked hesitantly to speak to Ann's husband, Jim. Although she never listened in on her doctor husband's conversations, her friend's nervous voice piqued Ann's curiosity. So when Jim picked up the phone in the back of the house, she stayed on the line. Her friend was stammering about terrible news on the radio. As she listened, Ann was struck that it was 6:30 A.M. in Georgia when the plane crashed.

Those scenes of eerie premonition, shock, horror, and incredulity reverberated all over the southeast. Each death was a personal tragedy, incomprehensible at first but soon a reality coming in electric jolts. Recalled in intricate detail as if it were a recent event—a phenomenon often resulting from sudden shock—each individual memory seems indelibly emblazoned on the mind. Inge Hill, who lived in Montgomery, Alabama, was twelve. He and his sister, Lee, were with their father at the family's lakeside retreat, and he had stayed awake most of the night, certain something was wrong. His mother, Frances Hill, grandmother, Clementina MacPherson, and aunt, Lee Virgin, were scheduled to return the next day on the Air France charter. After church, the family was playing putt-putt golf when a man summoned his father away. The somber conversation and grave expression on his father's face gave Inge the chilling realization that he had been right. Something terrible had happened.

Although airline crashes occurred frequently in 1962, the accident on June 3 was not like any of its predecessors. Never before had such a large group of leading citizens from one locale died in a single air disaster. In fact, never before had 130 people lost their lives in a single plane crash. First reports over WSB and WGST were sketchy and even the identity of the plane itself was uncertain. Before the days of instant satellite communication, news flashes traveled by telephone and overseas connections were painstakingly slow, so the early broadcasts were confusing, if not downright inaccurate. Mayor Ivan Allen later remembered that when he first heard the names of the passengers on the radio, the announcer mentioned someone he had just seen in Atlanta. Similarly, a man with the same name as somebody aboard the plane heard his own obituary.

Yet it was these fragmentary announcements that informed most Atlantans about the tragedy. Some like Teresa Turner intuited that it was the Art Association charter. When her radio-alarm roused her to go to Sunday school, through her sleepy fog she immediately knew that news of a plane crash meant her mother, Alee Tidmore, was dead. Her first impulse was to find her brother Bill, then living in their mother's house while attending Emory University. She would break the news gently by inviting him to stop by for breakfast. But when she reached him, it was too late. He had been listening to his car radio.

Linda Lanier also heard it unexpectedly on the radio. Visiting friends on the Chesapeake Bay, she was scheduled to be married the following Saturday in a chapel of Washington's National Cathedral. Nell and Tommy Lanier would be back from Europe just in time to attend the wedding and host a supper party. In Maryland with their friends, Linda and her fiancé were enjoying a leisurely Sunday morning with the radio playing in the background. Like so many others that same day, she heard about the Orly crash from a news flash that interrupted the regular broadcast.

In 1962, television was still in its infancy, yet breaking news bulletins did interrupt programs. These, however, came hours after the first radio announcements, so it was late morning before the Atlanta TV stations reported the crash. Twelve-year-old Tom Little was in his parents' bed watching cartoons. The phone rang and his aunt, who was staying with him, answered it while Tom listened silently on the upstairs extension. Another aunt was talking about the crash of an Air France Boeing 707 in Paris. Quickly Tom switched from the cartoons, searching for anything he could find about the crash. And that was how he heard the awful words "none of the passengers survived."

Others learned about it from relatives or friends, trying their best to break the tragic news gently. One of those was twenty-four-year-old Gregg Loomis. He and his then-wife had slept late that Sunday, June 3. It was a quiet respite their infant son rarely allowed. When the phone rang around nine, his wife answered and reported that his great-uncle Will Smith was saying that "there had been a problem" with the flight on which his sister Louise was scheduled to return. "Uncle Will was a perpetual prognosticator of ill-fortune," Gregg wrote in an unpublished memoir. Hadn't it been Uncle Will who advised the family to divest itself of Coca-Cola stock because coffee was a better investment? And Will had once even lamented that the family was making a dire mistake to own Atlanta real estate because Birmingham was destined to be a far larger and more prosperous city. Therefore, why pay attention to yet another prediction of doom and gloom from Uncle Will?

In about an hour, however, Gregg had a gnawing worry and decided he should call the Air France office to see what he could find out. The busy line delivered the first pangs of distress. When, after repeated dialing, he got through to a harassed woman with a heavy French accent, the horrible message was all too clear: "there had been an accident and there were no survivors."

Some people—either through an unconscious denial mechanism or through involuntary choice—could not or would not comprehend what they heard. When a close family friend shook Reese Lanier to wake him, he was totally baffled. He had been asleep only two hours and a voice was talking about the crash of an Air France Boeing 707. He had been enjoying one long party that reached a crescendo on the night of June 2, his graduation from Northside High School. To celebrate, he and a few friends arranged a party at Robinson's Tropical Garden, a popular teenage hangout on the banks of the Chattahoochee River. Around 6:30 A.M., he found himself on a girl's front porch when he remembered that he was scheduled to be at the airport that afternoon to pick up his parents. Only a few hours later at the friend's insistence, Reese retreated to his uncle Hicks Lanier's home to avoid the hoards of mourners going from house to house.

Audrey Goldstein now admits that she was in a state of denial when her husband Jake awakened her that Sunday morning to tell her the dreadful news about her sister and brother-in-law, Gladys and Arnold Kaye. "Why would you wake me up to tell me a crazy thing like that?" she murmured before turning over and going back to sleep. After Jake woke her up the second time, she was still protesting that it was not true, but at the same time urging that they get to her nephews right away because they were now responsible for them.

Bob Gerson was shaving when a friend called and told him in a solemn voice to turn on the radio. The news was bad, he said. Therefore when Micheline telephoned from Paris a few minutes later, he was unable to utter more than a word or two. It was too much to comprehend. Having originally planned to spend a leisurely Sunday before meeting his parents at the airport, Bob dressed hastily and rushed down to the Air France office. Along with numerous others, he tried frantically to learn more. What exactly had happened? Was everyone really dead? The news was totally overwhelming.

In some cases, hearing the news led to further tragedy. Dr. Marion Benson was making his rounds in the obstetrics ward at St. Joseph's hospital when someone told him that the plane upon which his wife, Sally, was scheduled to return had crashed. Overcome by grief, he returned to their Habersham Road home where he collapsed. Rushed to the emergency room, he was diagnosed as having suffered a cerebral hemorrhage. He never regained consciousness and died four days later.

Sally's son, Steve Clay, was finishing his sophomore year at Yale. On Sunday June 3, he had been riding motorcycles with a friend. When he returned to his dorm midmorning, he had a message from the campus police instructing him to call his uncle, Lucius Clay, then living in New York. General Clay told Steve about the crash and asked him to come at once to his Fifth Avenue apartment, making his nephew write down everything: the train schedule, the apartment number, and all the details, even though he had been there many times. "It turned out to be a good idea," Steve said later, "because I couldn't remember anything." Upon his arrival in New York, his uncle not only told him that the crash had no survivors, but also that his step-father had suffered a serious stroke. The general had already made reservations for Steve to return to Atlanta.

It was a Sunday in West Point, Georgia, and for Ann Cantey

that meant going to church. Her parents had the ritual so fixed in the family routine that even when they were away, Ann—who had just completed her freshman year at Randolph-Macon—attended services. After church, she had a big day ahead, having been delegated to drive Beth and Morgan Jr. to the Atlanta airport to meet their parents. A day or so earlier she had received a long letter from her father providing detailed instructions on finding the airport. Although she had driven there before, her father spelled out the route, told her to allow plenty of time for the seventy-nine mile journey, and warned her to fill the car with gas. "Please be extra careful on the drive up," Morgan Sr. had written, "because all I have will be in that car."

Beth was away with friends, so Ann rounded up young Morgan, made him put on his coat and tie, and took him along with her to the First Methodist Church. When they slid into the family pew, Ann felt "mounting tension" buzzing around the sanctuary as she "watched first one and then another adult" being "summoned" outside. "At communion," she remembered, "a white-knuckled minister was unable to say a prayer" over her or her brother. Worst of all, the usual after-church visitation had been mysteriously cancelled. Ann and Morgan were, in fact, whisked home. When they entered their house, it was filled with grim-faced people, and Ann remembered that "these unhappy adults" were trying hard to relay bad news. For a long time, she could not get them to answer the basic question she kept repeating: "Are they dead?"

When the truth finally came out, Ann went into the front yard, sank onto her knees, and screamed. The friends and neighbors, she recalled, "stood quietly on our front porch, never interrupting my initial reaction." Then she had the awful burden of telling Beth, who had just returned home. Within minutes, they both noticed their younger brother standing there. "Daddy said that, when he was gone, I was the man of the house," said ten-year-old Morgan. "What does a man of the house do when something like this happens?" Ann later realized: "That one clear moment was the beginning of the dealing—harder than hard so much of the time—confusing, frightening, awful and hopeless, but also comforting, reassuring and promising. Only in a small Southern town can one experience such an outpouring from people who care about you."

Within an hour, the Cantey home was filled with casseroles and baked goods. "What marvelous people!" Ann reflected. "Without them, I would have truly (and maybe permanently) crashed and burned. Each made the contribution for which they were best suited. And clearly none of them were going away as long as we needed anything."

East of West Point, in Elberton, Sam Patz got up early to listen to the crystal radio that he and his brother, Harry, had built. As they were aged twelve and eleven, it was the most extensive experiment they had ever undertaken, and they were amazed that the combination of old and new parts were really working. When Sam turned it on that June morning, an announcer was talking about a plane crash involving an Atlanta Art Association trip. Panicked, he told Harry what he had heard and then called a family friend. Apparently unaware of the accident, the man told Sam not to worry, it probably wasn't true. That afternoon, the two boys and their eight-year-old sister, Sarah Anne, were taken to visit friends, and when they returned home, they found a large crowd of people including their mother's sister from Chattanooga. "As a kid," wrote Sarah Anne, "it was a bizarre feeling walking past all those somber adults lining our hallway." Their aunt finally told them that the news Sam heard on the radio that morning was indeed true.

In Atlanta, the children of the Patzs' traveling companions

were experiencing the same pain that awful Sunday morning. Walt Crimm had celebrated his eighth birthday while his parents were away. Now they would be returning and the whole family would have a delayed party. In their Old Ivy Road home, Walt along with his twelve-year-old brother, Allan, and ten-year-old sister, Nina, had put up "Welcome Home" signs, and with the help of the sitter, they had baked a cake. Suddenly there was confusion. The family friend staying with them insisted that the three children go swimming very early in the morning. When they said they preferred to wait for their parents, she coaxed them into her Valiant and drove them to the Standard Club a few miles away.

After several hours and an obviously disturbing phone call, the sitter said it was time to go home. Cars were lining the street when they drove up and their living room was filled with people. The three children were taken into the den by their pediatrician and the rabbi. By that time, Nina was certain something awful had happened. But the adults were cautious. Not wanting to blurt out the truth, they decided to reveal the news gradually by saying that their parents were not coming back right away. Allan asked when that would be and one of the adults said it would be a long time. At that point, Nina began to scream: "They'll never be back, I know they'll never be back."

As the adults nodded somberly, Walt jumped up and ran to his parents' bathroom, barricading himself behind a locked door. Carefully, he opened the drawer where his father, Reuben, kept a collection of small soaps that he brought to the children when he returned from his travels. For a long time, Walt sat there tearfully unwrapping the small soaps. At least this was something belonging to his parents that he could hold onto. Knocks on the door finally persuaded him to unlock it, and then all three kids were told to rest in their own rooms. "We were all separated," said Walt wistfully. "We each felt so alone."

A few miles away on E. Beechwood Drive, Tom Little was sobbing. Within minutes of hearing the news on television, he dashed out of the house, not bothering to tell his aunt where he was going. Through the wooded yard he ran upward to a neighbor's house. When the neighbor intercepted him, he took one look at his tear-stained face and began teasing. Hurt and frightened, Tom finally got himself together enough to tell the man why he was crying. "And the neighbor just crumbled," Tom recalled.

At eighteen, Tom's sister Pat had been married for a little over a year and was the young mother of a three-month-old daughter. She and her nineteen-year-old husband were living in the basement apartment of her in-law's house. That morning, a relative had phoned to tell them about the crash, and Pat's first thought was to get to her younger brother as fast as she could. However, when she reached the house, Tom was nowhere to be found. Within a few minutes, the neighbor telephoned to report that he was with them. Pat dashed toward their house just as Tom started back home. They met in the woods and embraced. "I won't have to live with my aunt, will I?" the boy sobbed. "Please don't make me live with her."

Aubrey Morris, the news director for WSB radio, was attending Sunday services when a church usher summoned him because his wife was on the phone. King Elliott, the newsman on duty, had called him at home to tell him about the crash. Not waiting for the service to end, he rushed down to his office at White Columns, the WSB headquarters. There he consulted with his boss, Elmo Ellis, about the best way to report the tragedy.

No passenger lists had been released and only scraps of information were coming over the wires. Newsman King Elliott remained on the air, but could do little more than repeat the sketchy announcement. So Morris decided to go down to the Air France office on Forsyth Street and see if he could get a passenger list. The office was jammed with people, some in tennis shorts, some dressed for church. Among the crowd was Bob Gerson. "I had to come," he said, "just in case there was any other news." His parents had been "happy as kids" while they were in Europe he told a reporter. "Every time we heard from them they wrote how happy they were."

In fits and starts, names were spilling from the teletype machine and collecting in curled piles on the floor. It was the passenger list they had been awaiting. Morris was anxious to air the correct names, but he also realized that it was 11:00 A.M. and his station was due to broadcast from the First Presbyterian Church on Peachtree Road. However, in light of the unprecedented local tragedy, the pastor Dr. Harry Fifield announced from the pulpit that he was allowing Morris to preempt the service and read the complete list of passengers as it came over the wire.

Fifteen members of First Presbyterian had been on the plane, and Dr. Fifield had spent the past two hours consoling their relatives. Many in the congregation had already received the news either by radio or telephone, but others had not. So when the minister announced from the pulpit that there had been a terrible accident, an audible gasp echoed from pew to pew. Under the circumstances, Dr. Fifield made last minute changes in his sermon, so he could offer words of condolence and comfort to those listening to WSB. "There are a great many tragedies that strike us that we can't understand," he told the bereaved city. "We have the right to the conviction that any tragedy, even this one which has struck our community, can somehow in some way in God's hands find redemptive meaning."

Clergymen all over town that morning were offering similar prayers, and after services churchgoers congregated outside, talking softly in groups, comforting each other. Several planned official delegations to call on bereaved families in their congregations. Others set out on their own to go from house to house. Dour parades trudged up the driveways of north Atlanta. Men in dark suits with gray faces accompanied well-dressed women bearing steaming casseroles or trays of pastries.

Mayor Ivan Allen Jr.—who had been in office for only five months—was spending the weekend at the family farm in Franklin, Georgia, about seventy miles west of Atlanta. He was out in the meadow when one of the servants told him to call his wife. After Louise relayed the fragmentary report given to her by King Elliot, Allen said he felt as if he had been hit by "a Mack truck." It had been less than a month since he had seen the Atlantans depart from the airport. "If these early news reports were true," he remembered, "Atlanta was about to go through its greatest personal tragedy since General Sherman's visit."

He contacted his secretary Ann Moses, told her to open his office, and asked her to confirm the list of fatalities. Then he headed toward City Hall. On his rapid drive back to Atlanta, the mayor kept turning the radio dial, but even before he heard the official list, he understood that his social circle had been hit hard. "The first date I ever had was with Nancy Frederick, later Mrs. Robert Pegram," he recalled in the published account of his mayoralty. "One of my heaviest courtships during college days was with Louise Calhoun, later Mrs. Robby [sic] Robinson. These were my lifelong friends. This was my generation." They were "the backbone of Atlanta's cultural society, the city's leading patrons of the arts. There was no precedent for this kind of agony."

Unshaven and still wearing his khaki work clothes from the farm, Allen rushed into City Hall. His office was teeming with reporters, among them Aubrey Morris with the list of names copied from the Air France teletype. Phones were jangling with inquiries about people on the flight, as Ann Moses was frantically attempting to answer them. The mayor was "emotionally bushed," Aubrey Morris recollects. His own personal loss would have been weighty enough, but the responsibility of leading a city struck by a mutual tragedy was overwhelming.

His voice heavy with emotion, Allen told the covey of reporters that this was the greatest loss the city had ever experienced, and therefore, he was ordering flags lowered to half-staff and declaring a state of official mourning. Just as Atlanta was hoping to build "a great cultural center," he said wearily, "we have lost those who had given most towards the accomplishment of it." After the press conference ended, Allen remained dissatisfied. He knew those formalities were not enough. He would have to go to Paris, and after consulting with his staff, he arranged for his old friend, the associate city attorney Edwin L. Sterne, to accompany him. They booked two seats on the first available flight from New York, which happened to be an Air France Boeing 707. Then Allen realized that his passport had expired. Neither of Georgia's two senators, Herman Talmadge and Richard Russell, could be found, so the mayor decided to go directly to the State Department. Much to his relief, a woman on the other end of the line said he was cleared to travel all the way to Paris and would receive a new passport after his arrival.

Aubrey Morris left City Hall knowing that the focus of the news had shifted to the other side of the Atlantic, and he wanted to be in the heart of the action. When he got back to White Columns, he found a group of clergymen discussing their plans for memorial services. Finally he was able to pull Ellis aside and boldly announce: "I'm going to Paris." Without hesitation, Ellis agreed and set the wheels in motion to expedite his departure.

In 1962, no system for crisis news coverage existed. No overseas reporters were stationed abroad to transmit breaking news via satellite. There was no such thing as video and audio tapes, nor camcorders, nor e-mails and faxes. Written reports came across teletype and telegraph wires, often discordant and difficult to read. Bulky cameras were awkward and required expert handling; and reel-to-reel films were not only slow to process but could only be transmitted by the next available plane. Morris and Ellis both knew that the only way to get the story back to Atlanta was to have an experienced man on the spot to telephone reports. The intrepid Aubrey Morris fit the bill. WSB would take care of all expenses, Ellis assured his news director, even his pocket money. Then Morris called his wife, who gathered a few of his clothes and transported them to White Columns.

A few blocks down Peachtree Street from WSB, the Atlanta Art Association was in mournful hysterics. Suddenly it had become a center of frenetic activity. Ordinarily the museum galleries were closed on Sunday, but now the red-brick building was alive with volunteers manning telephones, some sobbing as they spoke with concerned friends and inquiring strangers. Telegrams from around the world had been arriving all afternoon. One was from President and Mrs. John F. Kennedy, another from Martin Luther King Jr. The White House—which was receiving messages from Charles de Gaulle, Pope John XXIII, German Chancellor Konrad Adenauer, and other world leaders—was rapidly transmitting all communications to Atlanta. Someone would have to answer all of these, but it seemed that every volunteer who would have ordinarily been writing such letters had just perished at Orly. Sometime in the middle of the afternoon, a large wreath of white lilies appeared at the front door of the museum. The flag in front flew at half-staff, and a stricken guard stood beside the entrance.

When he heard about the crash, *Constitution* editor Eugene Patterson came down to his office. He probably would have been there anyway, because he needed to prepare for a scheduled trip to France the next day. Earlier in the year, he had been invited to travel with other media officials to view American military bases abroad, and he was scheduled to leave for Paris on June 4 aboard an Air France Boeing 707.

Before departing from Atlanta, Mayor Allen held another news conference, again assuring the city that he would strive to do everything in his power to investigate the causes of the crash, identify the bodies, and expedite their return. When he, Sterne, and Morris were settled aboard the Delta plane headed for New York, the WSB news director warned Allen to be prepared for aggressive New York journalists waiting at Idlewild Airport. They were different, he explained, from the polite Southerners he knew at home. And sure enough, thirty-five or forty of what both Morris and Allen described as "New York types" with cameras flashing were edging their way forward, engulfing the three Atlantans accustomed to a more gentle type of media coverage.

The mayor later recalled that Morris, "a good ol' boy" who "could get in there and punch with the best of them, handled his peers as handsomely as possible." In turn, Morris remarked that the mayor fielded the barrage of questions amazingly well. Allen said he did not want to comment on causes of the crash before he was able to appraise the situation, nor would he reveal his expectations about what they might find in Paris. He merely told reporters that the Atlantans were going to France to represent the city and relay their findings to the bereaved families at home. It was nearly 10 P.M. when Allen, Sterne, and Morris left the impromptu press conference and shuttled across Idlewild Airport to the Air France Terminal. Shortly afterward, they boarded the Boeing 707 that would take them to Paris.

Stunned silence pervaded Atlanta that same Sunday night. Crowds milled around downtown waiting to buy a special edition of the *Atlanta Journal*. Along the sidewalks of Forsyth and Marietta Streets, people stared at each other, some crying openly, others tearing up silently as they reeled off the names of people they had known. "I just got a card from Rosalind Williams," said one man who worked with her at Tucker-Wayne Advertising. "She said they had had a wonderful time on the tour." Another remarked that Christopher McLoughlin had been his doctor for the past fifteen years; another commented that Winifred Paige had been a member of her sorority. Others remembered Baxter Jones, Morris Brandon, Roy and Ella Bixler. One woman commented that she was a member of the Atlanta Art Association and knew many of those killed. "This means we will all have to pull together," she said. "It will take time, lots of time to recover from this loss."

Reese Lanier remembers being at the home of his Uncle Sot on the evening of June 3. An announcer was reading the passenger list on the radio, and his parents' names were not on it. He knew, however, that they would never have changed their plans with his sister's wedding scheduled for the next weekend. He was also sure that his father, who had never been away from work for such a long time, was "crawling the walls" to get back to the office. Despite his gut feelings that they had been on the flight, Reese wanted to be certain. So he joined the crowd downtown waiting for the special edition of the *Journal*. Scanning the complete passenger list, his eyes rested on "Thomas and Nell Lanier."

CHAPTER 12

❧ *Grief and Coping*

O
n the Air France jet flying over the ocean on the
night of June 3, Mayor Allen, Aubrey Morris, and Ed
Sterne were wide awake. Not only were they unac-
customed to the roar of the jet engines, but they were overwhelmed by the enormity of their task. For most of the night,
the mayor and his lawyer talked over what they hoped to accomplish the following day. Sterne explained that Allen had
"absolutely no authority outside the city limits of Atlanta," and
would be at the mercy of the French government. They were
"running on emotional energy," Morris remembered. At one
point, Allen was invited to visit the cockpit and requested that
his newsman come along. The mayor is "a very inquisitive individual," said Morris. Jet travel was something new and he wanted
to see how the Boeing 707 worked. The world of 1962 had no

concept of terrorism and any curious passenger could get permission to visit the captain at the controls.

Ironically, the mayor's plane landed on runway 26 where the zigzag black skid marks from the previous day's accident were jarringly visible. When the Atlantans arrived at Orly, two gendarmes came aboard the plane and announced that no passengers could leave until Allen and his party departed. Jet-lagged and emotionally overwrought, the Atlantans stumbled down the metal stairs, only to encounter an official French delegation of twenty-five or thirty people wearing striped trousers and frock coats. Led by the mayor of Paris, the party included an emissary of President Charles de Gaulle, the French Minister of Aviation, and representatives of Air France.

In the memoir of his years as mayor, Allen commented: "I realized how insignificant I was, but I knew I had to assume the posture of representing those families and, indeed, the entire city of Atlanta, Georgia." He admitted knowing "nothing about protocol, foreign relations, aviation, international agreements, or any of the other details" that he would have to face and realized that he was "nothing but the mayor of Atlanta and a friend and neighbor of 106 people who had been killed at this same airport, only the day before." Aware that he was an envoy of his city, Allen recalled: "I threw my shoulders back and sucked in my stomach and talked myself into summoning all of the dignity and restraint I could find. I would represent those families to the best of my ability." Then they asked Allen to meet with reporters at the airport. "It was the largest press conference I confronted in my eight years in the mayor's office," he recalled ten years later. "All of the international press was there. I had no proof of the nature of the accident so didn't try to belabor the point about who might have been at fault."

Immediately, they were taken to the crash site. Wearing hard hats, the Atlanta contingent toured the remains of the fractured jet. Morris reported to Atlanta that "Mayor Allen and Attorney Edwin Sterne appeared stunned as they walked among the smoldering wreckage." In the distance they could see the tail section which had been blown several hundred feet, allowing the two stewardesses to escape unharmed. Suitcases had opened and spilled all their contents, some charred, some intact: a mink stole with a J.P. Allen label, a cocktail dress, a harmonica, an opera program, a souvenir booklet, two dolls. As they sifted through the ashes, the mayor said he recognized a necktie that he had given a friend for Christmas and the piece of a dress that he had seen Nancy Pegram wearing earlier that year.

French authorities had required all reporters and photographers to remain at a distance beyond a fence ringed with gendarmes. With a journalist's eye, Morris understood he would have to change that restriction, and he eventually convinced the mayor that if he wanted the people in Atlanta to know for certain that he had visited the scene of the accident, he would need photographs. Since no American television reporters or cameramen were present, they had to rely on the French. Working through interpreters, Allen asked permission to bring the reporters closer. Within minutes, a horde of camera-toting media personnel descended on the scene, snapping many of the photos that would be flown to the United States in time for the evening news and next day's papers.

Atlanta Constitution editor, Eugene Patterson, who arrived in Paris the following morning, also visited the crash site. Already scheduled to be in France that day visiting military installations, he found himself covering a much more difficult story. In flight, Patterson identified himself and explained that he been an Army pilot during World War II. The Air France captain, therefore, allowed him to sit beside him in the cockpit as the plane approached Orly. Although their flight did not land on Runway 26, the pilot pointed out the scarred concrete pitted by the curved trail left by the burning tires. "The tail section of the 707 was still sitting among the acacia and ash trees," Patterson observed.

The Atlanta editor visited Villeneuve-le-Roi twice that day as French gendarmes were raking through the ashes looking for jewelry and valuables. "I walked around the great burned tail," Patterson remembered, "and off in the grass on the edge of the rubble, I picked up a small yellow can of 35 mm film which had been exposed. The can itself was scorched." Wondering whether the photographs could be saved, he dropped it into his pocket to be developed at the newspaper when he returned. He also found a "half-burned booklet" that "was obviously high quality" and he attempted to decipher the French but was unable to read a word, even though he was vaguely familiar with the language. Assuming that it had been purchased in France by one of the doomed passengers, he asked the manager of his hotel to translate it, but the Frenchman also found it baffling. Finally they consulted an expert, who concluded that it must be medieval French in a form that no one could read sufficiently. Although neither Patterson nor anyone else knew it then, that booklet was probably one of the treasures purchased by Paul Barnett as he rambled through Paris.

Before the days of sophisticated digital voice recorders, there was no way to determine exactly what the crew was doing moments before the plane crashed. Only a thorough examination of the wreckage could determine the causes, and then—as today—that kind of inquiry required many months of intensive study before a final report could be issued. The Orly tragedy was the fourth such incident in the past sixteen months involving a Boeing 707. Two had happened shortly before the June 3 crash.

Ninety-five people died in March 1962, when an American Airlines 707 nose-dived just after take-off from New York's Idlewild Airport. Two months later, a Continental 707 disintegrated near Centerville, Iowa, during an electrical storm, killing all forty-five people aboard. A little over a year before that, in February 1961, seventy-two people died when a Sabena 707 spun out of control when circling for a landing in Brussels. The press was quick to report that something seemed wrong with the Boeing jet, then the most frequently used transcontinental and transoceanic carrier.

Shortly after the Air France charter burst into flames, a Paris representative of the CAB (Civil Aeronautics Board) was on the scene. However, the American predecessor of the FAA (Federal Aviation Agency) would not be conducting the investigation alone because the accident occurred on French soil and the plane was owned and operated by the French government. Thus the CAB—which was already in the process of scrutinizing the three recent Boeing 707 crashes—named George Haldeman of its Bureau of Safety to head the American team in the international inquiry.

The first step in the investigation was a formal inquest. Air France handled the situation very well, Aubrey Morris remembered. "They had a public relations disaster on their hands," so they simply said inquiries were underway. Official inquests had to take place within the department in which the accident occurred. That meant that on June 4, shortly after they inspected the crash site, the Atlanta delegation was ushered to what Morris described as the French equivalent of a "dinky county courthouse" in the town of Villeneuve-le-Roi. A coroner read the official cause of the deaths to legally certify what happened in anticipation of future suits. Instead of resenting Mayor Allen's presence at the inquest, Aubrey Morris commented, the French officials were grateful he was there. To them he was a sounding board as well as a spokesperson. Edwin Sterne reminded Allen that officially he had no authority. And thus the Atlantans listened attentively but made few comments.

As has become common practice after a major catastrophe, numerous unofficial—and generally false—speculations on the causes of the crash proliferated. The most widespread implied that too many passengers, too much luggage, and an over-supply of fuel prevented the jet from lifting off the ground. Others blamed Boeing. More knowledgeable individuals knew it was more complicated than that. Two experienced men, both officers in the U.S. Navy, had intimate connections with the crash victims. Lt. Commander William Dilts was a Navy pilot assigned to the Air Defense Command in New York; and Captain William Hunnicutt was commanding a destroyer squadron sailing with the Sixth Fleet.

When Dilts learned about the crash from a friend's telephone call, he went immediately to the Air France office at Idlewild to make certain that his mother, Mildred, had been on the plane. Earlier she had told him that she, Allee Tidmore, and Ruby Adair might leave the trip and go to Spain. But after he found their names on the passenger list, he decided to go at once to Paris. As an aviation safety officer in the Navy, his job involved investigating accidents. But Dilts soon discovered that getting to France would not be as easy as he thought. For one thing, he needed a passport, and when he tried to get assistance from the State Department, he was told it would take several days. In frustration, he called Senator Herman Talmadge. A few hours later, he had the passport and left New York on the evening of June 4.

Captain Hunnicutt—who along with his wife Barron had celebrated his brother-in-law Tom Lanier's birthday in Portofino a week earlier—was aboard the Independence off the coast of Italy when he heard news of the crash. At once he began making travel arrangements. On the morning after the accident, he boarded a Navy plane on the carrier, flew to Rome, and transferred to the civilian airport so he could get an Alitalia flight to Paris. In advance he found out that Ivan Allen, Aubrey Morris, and Ed Sterne were staying at the Hôtel de Crillon on the Place de la Concorde adjacent to the American Embassy, so he booked a room there. When he arrived at the hotel that evening, he called on the mayor and received a report detailing what the Atlantans had seen at the crash site. He told them he would be going there the following day.

That evening Mayor Allen reported to the *Atlanta Constitution* that the visit to Paris was "the most difficult job" he had done in a long time. Heading the lead article on the front page of the Tuesday paper was a photograph of Allen inspecting the wreckage, arranged because Aubrey Morris had summoned the cameramen. It was "a most grief-laden task and a very sorrowful journey," the mayor said.

On Tuesday morning, June 5, Mayor Allen, Aubrey Morris, and Ed Sterne walked over to the United States Embassy next to their hotel. Morris had been in the building a year earlier on a tour of journalists receiving information about the Atlantic Alliance. General James Gavin, United States Ambassador to France in 1962, was then the commander of NATO briefing the visiting American reporters. Morris, therefore, felt he had an inside edge over his Atlanta companions. Not only had he recently met and interviewed the ambassador, but he had worked with his press secretary. Allen later teased him about his familiarity with the embassy. "Morris came in and took over the meeting" the mayor jibed. "He came right up and put his foot in the ambassador's chair, picked up the ambassador's phone and commanded: 'Get me WSB in Atlanta!'"

The broadcaster had actually sought the assistance of the embassy staff with a reporter's expertise, although not as brashly as the mayor later implied. Just before their official visit, Morris had requested use of the direct line to the State Department to relay a message from Washington to Atlanta. But when he tried to get a statement from Gavin, the ambassador replied: "No comment." So the quick-thinking newsman asked: "Well, if you did have a comment, what would it be?" Morris therefore got his quote, which he transmitted by phone in time for a live broadcast on WSB.

After the Atlantans met with Ambassador Gavin, they made arrangements to return to Villeneuve-le-Roi with embassy officials. Bill Hunnicutt happened to be at the embassy that morning requesting permission for a similar trip. When he ran into the mayor's party, Morris asked the captain to go along with them as a direct representative of the victims' families. Again cameramen were on hand to take photographs of Hunnicutt and Allen touring the scene. Like everyone else who visited the site, Hunnicutt was struck by the complete disintegration of the large Boeing 707 and the widely scattered fragments of airplane parts as well as luggage and personal belongings. He took notes and drew sketches and later compiled it as a report to send back to Atlanta. "There was no fuselage as such nor even seats," he wrote, "but rather bits of molten aluminum, wreckage, pieces of cloth, shoes and general destruction. . . . The soot and ashes made the area black, yet there were inexplicable pieces of unburned clothing, a silk scarf almost undamaged."

As for the causes of the crash, Hunnicutt repeated what others had concluded about the pilot's hasty decision to abort and reverse the thrust of the jet engines. He added that Hoche apparently turned off the engines in an attempt to prevent fire, but the plane was already so damaged by having its fuel tanks punctured that the explosion was inevitable. "Doubtless something caused the pilot to decide to abort the flight," Hunnicutt commented. It was "perhaps a realization that some control was not operative or some similar factor." But the likelihood of it being caused by excess weight, he believed, was highly unlikely.

Upon his return to Paris, Bill Hunnicutt had to face the most difficult part of his mission: the attempt to identify the bodies of his sister, her husband, and their traveling companions. It was at this point that he met up with Bill Dilts, who had just arrived from New York. They soon discovered that the French had severe restrictions against allowing uninvited persons to view remains. Suddenly the two men realized that both were wearing civilian clothes and therefore getting nowhere. When they changed into their officer's uniforms, they had no problem being admitted into the morgues and hospitals.

It was a gruesome task that Mayor Allen, Ed Sterne, and Aubrey Morris had undertaken on the day they arrived. Paris lacked the facilities to house so many bodies at once, and thus the remains of the crash victims were scattered about in four or five different locations. Because of the severity of the explosion and lack of any means of identifying the passengers, the bodies of couples were often in different locations. When they made their grim rounds, the mayor's party was accompanied by an official of the State Department's consular service and Atlanta banker, Harvey Hill, who happened to be in Paris vacationing with his wife.

One of the morgues, Aubrey Morris remembered, was in the heart of the city adjacent to a chilly cave where they stored the bodies. He was struck that in the twentieth century, the French still relied on medieval means of preservation. Mayor Allen had pledged to see every one of the victims so he could assure their relatives in Atlanta that he had viewed them all. It involved a long and wearing process because authorities would only allow them to inspect one body at a time. As they removed sheet after sheet, the mayor could only look and shake his head. Originally hoping to help identify some of them, he was unable to certify any of the charred remains, thus becoming jarringly aware that this would be a job for forensic experts.

Micheline Tindel did not have the same experience. When she went from morgue to morgue in search of her future in-laws, she found their remains in separate places. They looked sunburned, she said, but were easy to recognize. Saul Gerson even had the wrapper in his hand from the candy that the flight crew had just dispensed. Bill Dilts corroborated Micheline's observations. The conditions of the bodies, Dilts said, varied tremendously. Those in the front section of the plane probably "died of asphyxiation," because one could hardly "tell they had been hurt." Others were completely disfigured.

After visiting three or four morgues with Bill Hunnicutt at his side, Dilts found his mother's remains, which he was able to recognize because of three Caesarian scars on her abdomen and a charm bracelet containing the names of his own children. Although Hunnicutt had more trouble finding his sister and Carroll Young, he was able to identify Tommy Lanier and Sykes Young. In addition to finding a wallet in his brother-in-law's pocket, the captain found the cuff links he had been wearing at their birthday celebration in Portofino, still clamped into the shirt cuff. Despite those few successes, the rest of the bodies were hard to distinguish, and everyone who viewed the bodies realized that the identification process was bound to be long and tedious.

Before they were done, Dilts and Hunnicutt delivered the list of passengers to the Mayor of Villeneuve le Roi. By law, the death certificates must bear the name of the exact location in which the crash occurred. In order to prepare those certificates, the French government required that each one contain the date and place of birth. The two men provided that information for their own relatives. But for the rest, such details had to be obtained through the American consular service. Later the two officers, accompanied by a member of the embassy staff, went to look through the personal effects held in a baggage collection and accident analysis station near Versailles. Hunnicutt was able to find his sister's passport, a wallet containing photographs of her children, and the Florentine pitcher that Nell Lanier had given Tommy for his birthday.

While Mayor Allen and his entourage were meeting with dignitaries and viewing the remains, plans were underway for a memorial service at the American Cathedral in Paris. The Gothic-revival structure on the avenue George V—with its bell tower and cloistered courtyard—was founded in 1886 by the Episcopal Church as a sanctuary for Americans abroad. Through two world wars, the elaborate stone edifice served as a center for interdenominational worship and that spirit dominated the service to commemorate those lost in the Orly crash.

On the morning of Wednesday, June 6, 1962, two members of the Veterans of Foreign Wars stood at the cathedral's entrance, each holding an American flag. Mounted above the raised pulpit was another flag, flanked on either side by gold crosses and menorahs. Inside the vaulted sanctuary, a stony-faced mayor edged into the front-row pew. It was the eighteenth anniversary of D-Day, and Ambassador James Gavin was attending a ceremony in Normandy. But sitting next to Allen to represent the U.S. government were Minister Cecil Lyon and Consul-General Herbert Fales.

Gathered in the cathedral were around 500 mourners from

Europe and the United States. A large French contingent attended, many of them relatives of lost crew members; others were Air France employees and sympathetic Parisians. One of the French families was that of Paul Dossans, the Air France manager who died with the passengers he was shepherding. Micheline Tindel and her parents were also there. In addition to Dilts and Hunnicutt, Max and Mildred Seydel—whose brother Vasser Woolley was among those lost—were attending. And many Atlantans were also in the cathedral, some coming to Paris from various parts of Europe where they had been vacationing.

After the congregation sang "O God, Our Help in Ages Past," Dean Sturgis L. Riddle of the American Cathedral, draped in purple and white ecclesiastical robes, opened the service with a prayer. Participating in the readings were Rabbi Robert Weiler, an Air Force chaplain wearing his dress blue uniform; Dr. Clayton E. Williams, minister of the American Church in Paris; and Father Thomas Cowley of the Dominican Institute of Ecumenical Studies in Paris. Then after the hymn, "God Be In My Head," Dean Riddle climbed up to the pulpit to deliver the eulogy. Hunnicutt described the Episcopalian clergyman as being "a tall dignified man, of about sixty-five with great horn-rim glasses that add to his scholarly and churchly mien." In "deliberate and sonorous" tones he pronounced: "These fellow Americans were united with us in the bond of the spirit. They were lovers of art, pilgrims to shrines of beauty in this old world which now with us wears the badge of sorrow."

Ending the service was a dramatic choir rendition of "Libera Me Domine" from Gabriel Fauré's *Requiem,* accompanied by chords from a thundering organ sending echoes that reverberated through the stone sanctuary. Then in striking contrast the church bells gently chimed the military salute to the dead, known as "Taps" before the final hymn, "Nearer My God to

Thee." Mayor Allen led the solemn recessional, his drawn face reflecting the strain of his three-day mission. After the service, Allen, Sterne, and Morris were hustled into a limousine and rushed to Orly so they could board their flight back to the United States.

When the exhausted mayor arrived at the Atlanta airport that evening, he held a hasty news conference to recapitulate what had transpired in Paris. Earlier in the day, he said, he had asked Consul General Fales to see that the remains be sent home individually in labeled caskets. On the next afternoon, Allen met at City Hall with relatives of the deceased. To his stricken audience, the mayor reported that he had viewed every one of the bodies and felt fairly certain that most would be returned within the next month. He also requested that the families aid the FBI investigation by providing as many details as possible, including dental records and medical histories along with descriptions of jewelry and other personal effects. Thus began a dreadful search that haunted so many of the bereaved.

With no bodies to bury, Atlanta churches and synagogues held a series of memorial services, some group commemorations and requiem masses, others in memory of specific individuals or families. So many members of St. Phillips Episcopal Cathedral, Christ the King Catholic Cathedral, and the First Presbyterian Church had died, that those sanctuaries were overflowing with mourners. Many were photographed kneeling outside the main entrances. Memorial eulogies and prayers similar to the ones spoken in Paris interspersed with booming organ recitations resounded around the city. Having lost thirteen of its members, the Junior League held its own service in the ballroom of the Piedmont Driving Club.

Although relatives of those killed remember in minute detail where they had been when receiving the shocking news of the crash, the weeks that followed were a nightmarish blur. Most people vaguely recall a similar pattern of occurrences. Formal telegrams and letters from city and state officials along with similar documents from the French government arrived at each home. With no formal framework for dealing with such loss, friends were also having a hard time coping with the tragedy. Mary Elizabeth Schroder remembers that everyone was "sympathizing with each other," and "the pain of the whole thing" seemed all consuming. "It was a time of so much shock that those of us who remained alive were wounded, bruised on all sides," Doris Lockerman commented. After the condolence calls and memorial commemorations ended, the individual families were left with the agony of waiting for the bodies to be returned. In frustration, some people demanded immediate action. The sons of Annette Snelson Payne, for example, announced that they were suing Air France for $250,000. But a few days later, when cooler heads prevailed, the Paynes realized that their suit was premature and they withdrew it. In most cases the frustration took a more private and devastating course.

After the mayor asked each family to produce dental records and fill out forms specifying physical attributes of the deceased, many households became the scenes of extensive FBI searches. Carroll Young recalled that the agent who came looking for specific clothing and shoe sizes was a "big, tough looking man with a well-trained, gentle, and polite manner." Pat Little Reynolds remembers that when the FBI knocked on their door, she had to spend an entire afternoon describing her parents scars and ended up giving them photographs so they could study the bone structures.

Jane Greene had a "terrible time" complying with everything the investigators wanted. Because Ruby Stow had only one kidney, Jane thought her body would be easy to identify. Nevertheless the FBI asked for additional means of identification in addition to medical and dental records, so she had to measure her mother's clothes. Then weeks passed and no word. Finally, Jane grew so disgusted that she contacted Senator Talmadge, whom she knew personally. Two days later her mother's body came back. Others simply waited.

Not only had Ivan Allen laid down strict instructions for making certain that each body would be correctly identified, but the French required extensive paper work in each case, all causing considerable delays. All the while, packages and postcards from the deceased continued to arrive. Weeks after the crash, Gregg Loomis received an Austrian ski sweater, which he still prizes, a hand-carved chess set, and six colored Venetian glasses. "The experience of receiving these items was, well, macabre," he remarked. Some of the packages delivered to relatives and friends were obvious gifts, others were the items mailed separately to avoid paying duty.

From the end of June until the middle of August, long-awaited phone calls from the French Government informed family members they could retrieve the remains of their loved ones at the Atlanta Airport. Each one arrived in a delicately carved, small octagon-shaped casket bearing a simple brass plate inscribed with the name. Many of the relatives commented on the beauty of the "old fashioned" oak coffins. Loomis remembered viewing his sister's casket at Patterson's Funeral Home, and, although he greatly admired the French craftsmanship, the experience was "an event not unlike peeling the scab from a particularly painful wound."

As the remains returned, a new round of services took place. For many of the survivors, the burials were a final closure to an event which had caused so much agony. One man said that as he was standing at Westview Cemetery burying his mother, he looked across the road and recognized people attending a similar graveside service. Only then did he fully realize that the whole community was suffering.

After all the bodies came back, the Allen administration asked family members and executors of estates to identify personal items at the downtown branch of the Carnegie Library. Lined up on tables in the basement were bags of jewelry, a prayer book, a crucifix, cigarette lighters, rolls of film, cameras, glasses, wallets, purses, and even molten jewelry. Individuals wandered around the tables, identifying some things and jotting down what they had found. Many remembered the place to be cold and depressing and the gruesome task of viewing remnants of once-vibrant people to be excruciatingly painful.

While Atlantans were burying their loved ones, Susan Coltrane was trying to deal with her own grief as she traveled alone through Austria. During the time that she was touring with the Art Association group, she had received postcards from Mason Lowance at each stop along the way. After hearing about the crash, he called her in Innsbruck and advised her to come immediately to England. But still in shock and terribly uncertain about what to do next, she decided to complete her planned trip. She did telephone the Hôtel Crillon to speak with Edwin Sterne and Mayor Allen, explaining that she was in Europe and wanted to be helpful in any way that she could—but because of that communication the press found her. The first calls that came from news magazines were so insensitive that she refused to talk with any representatives of the press.

While trying to complete her pre-planned trip, Susan became suddenly aware how much she longed to speak her native language and see familiar faces from home. Consequently, she abandoned her original plans and flew immediately to England. She remained in London for awhile, before making her way to Oxford and checking into the Randolph Hotel. Several of Mason's friends from Princeton were then studying at the university and Susan ended up doing "tons of sightseeing" with them. The sojourn, therefore, turned out to be very restorative.

The rest of the tale has a storybook ending. Susan Coltrane returned to Atlanta in mid-October, and when Mason Lowance finished his studies at Oxford, they became engaged and have remained happily married ever since. Their romance is perhaps the one and only silver lining for a European tour that turned into tragedy.

CHAPTER 13

❧ *Survival and Commemoration*

The lines of cars visiting home after home in the vicinity of Buckhead tells the story. As one person phrased it: "Atlanta was knocked to its knees by the crash." So many families were bereaved, that for several weeks the city seemed paralyzed. One of the most jarring losses was the demise of Fred Bull's entire family: himself, his wife, two daughters, his mother, and his uncle. In an editorial written en route to Paris, Eugene Patterson remembered driving past their two-story brick house on Westover Drive. Mrs. Bull, he wrote, "had one of those fine, good faces that are more than just beautiful because there was a lighting of inward warmth and grace. Their two children were pretty girls. . . . The house on Westover is empty. It is asking a bit much of a person or a city to absorb the loss that Sunday's crash inflicted on Atlanta. From the small remembrances will come a full grasp finally. The thing happened so quickly and so far away, and it injured Atlanta so deeply, that it is still hard to believe."

The sudden deaths affecting one community were staggering. The city, neither before nor since, had seen anything like it. Thirty-three individuals aged twenty-one and under were orphaned; twenty others in that age group lost their mothers. Forty-six adults lost one or both parents; nineteen men and two women lost their spouses; five sets of parents, fifteen widowed mothers, and six fathers lost their children. At least 104 people lost siblings. Many—like the Bevingtons, Blacks, Bealers, Berrys, Hills, and Virgins—were mourning more than one family member.

Hardest hit were the orphaned children, especially those between ages eight and eighteen. Losing both parents during those formative years meant irrevocable alterations of comfortable daily routines. Most of the children were relocated to live with relatives or friends; a few remained at home under the supervision of a family member. In the days before psychological counseling was recommended in such cases, adults encouraged youngsters not to mention their deceased parents and to "get on with life." It was often too painful for the guardians to be constantly reminded of their own losses, and many of those inheriting young children or adolescents had no previous experience in child rearing. In some cases the guardianships worked, in others it was traumatic.

Allan, Nina, and Walt Crimm experienced the latter. When Reuben changed his will on the way to the airport, leaving his maiden sister Rosalene as guardian, the children were thrown into a melee of personal isolation and inner-family squabbling. Prior to moving in with the Crimm children, Rosalene had been living with her mother and was only a distant figure in their lives. Now suddenly she took over their house and became their sole custodian. The adjustment was difficult for them all. The children lost contact with families that had been Reuben and Jan's friends and felt cut off from the world that their active and involved parents had provided. "All of a sudden I became an adult, a survivor," Nina said. "My whole attitude in life was survival. We didn't have real family anymore around. Atlanta disappeared."

Other orphaned youngsters were more fortunate. The three children of Baxter and Julia Jones were adopted by Julia's brother, Bates Block and his wife Margaret. Because the Blocks had no children, they raised young Julia (almost eleven), Baxter (five) and Douglas (two) as if they were their own. They built a new house and tried as much as humanly possible to create a warm and comfortable environment. Frania Lee adopted her grandson, Ronny Cartledge, who was then only three and gave him the security of a loving household.

Morgan and Ted Cantey's children also found a welcoming home. The small town of West Point was itself comforting with friends and neighbors converging to help Ann (nineteen), Beth (sixteen), and Morgan Jr. (twelve). A young couple, H.E. and Carolyn (Buddie) Steele, immediately took charge of the Cantey children and moved them into their house. Buddie was only fourteen years older than Ann and although they knew Morgan Sr. and Ted, the age difference meant they were only casual friends. "They simply decided that their contribution to the world would be to share their family with three other children," Ann remembers. Their own children were small and suddenly they had two adolescents and a college student to deal with. "We instantly *became* their children in every sense of the word, " Ann commented. "They paid our allowances, purchased our clothes and other essentials, attended our various parents' meetings and football games, carpooled Beth and Morgan and propped eyes open to stay awake long enough to enforce curfew."

The Patz children did not have the Canteys' advantage of remaining in a small town, although they remember Elberton with great affection. Sam, then twelve, was sent to Baltimore to live with his uncle, Dr. Arnall Patz and his wife Ellen. Dr. Patz would become chairman of the Ophthalmology department at the Johns Hopkins University and that close association with the medical world was to affect Sam's life. Harry (eleven) and Sarah Anne (eight) went to Chattanooga to the home of their mother's sister. The Patz offspring never forgot Elberton and the feeling was apparently mutual. Several days after the accident, the town held a memorial service for Louis and Florette in a large hall that was filled to overflowing; the rabbi from Athens presided. Shortly afterward, Elberton named its small airport Patz Field in memory of the family that contributed so much to the community. Similarly, the Georgia Jewish community memorialized the Patzs with a plaque in the Athens synagogue where Louis, Florette, and their family worshipped.

Other children orphaned by the crash went to the homes of relatives. Three of Betty and David Murphy's children lived in Atlanta with their aunt and uncle, John Francis Carver and his wife Mildred, who had two daughters of their own. At the time David Murphy Jr. was fourteen, Michael about ten, and Elizabeth a few years younger. Their half-brother, Chris Grabbe, then college age, moved in with his paternal grandmother. Both his biological father and now his mother and step-father had been killed in plane crashes. Randy and Chris Berry, who were approximately thirteen and eleven when their parents died, went to live with their uncle Henry Berry and his wife Nancy in Rome, north of Atlanta.

Audrey and Jake Goldstein were the guardians of their nephews, Beau and Rick Kaye. Immediately after the crash they moved into Arnold and Gladys's Sandy Springs home, but when they got matters settled there, they took the boys, then aged fourteen and sixteen, to their apartment near Emory. At the time, both boys were attending Georgia Military Academy (later Woodward Academy). Jake remembers: "They had a hard time. They lost so much, they lost their home, their hobbies, lost the animals, everything was gone."

Beau Kaye, the oldest, longed to return to his former neighborhood. After a short time with his aunt and uncle, he moved in with a friend and attended Sandy Springs High School. After one more move into another home in the area, Beau graduated from high school and enrolled in the University of Georgia. But there, too, he dropped in and out until he finally pulled himself together and received a law degree. Rick made a slightly better adjustment. "But when he reached the point that he could legally choose," his aunt said, "he moved in with his grandparents." Barney and Jenny Kaye lived north of Buckhead, and while Rick lived there, he finished high school and went on to Oglethorpe University. During those years, his grandmother died, and through her long illness and after her death, he and his grandfather became very close.

Tom Little Jr. was among the more fortunate. His sister Pat, along with her husband and baby, moved back into their parents' home. Although she was only eighteen, Pat knew she wanted to take charge of her twelve-year-old brother, even though several of their older relatives continued to question her ability to bring up an adolescent. But Tom never doubted her capabilities. "It ended up that was my family," he said. Before their parents' death they were a typical sister and brother with all of the teasing and bickering. But after the crash, they drew together. "I never considered myself an orphan," Tom remarked. "Over the years it was a wonderful relationship. I feel very fortunate in that regard."

Jane McLoughlin's mother, Deryl Sharp, lived with the family in their Hillside Drive home. She was there with Chris (eighteen) and Norman (thirteen) when they heard about the crash, and they remained in her home until they grew up. Their legal guardian, however, was their uncle, Jack Sharp, who remained close to his nephews while trying to care for his mother, who was so devastated by the loss of her daughter that she never fully stopped grieving. When his parents died, Chris had just finished his freshman year at the University of Georgia and began focusing his life on college.

Reese Lanier was entering Georgia as a freshman that year, and although he was away from home most of the time, the loss of his parents did cause immediate changes. As planned, Linda married on the Sunday following the crash, but the wedding at the National Cathedral was exchanged for a small, private ceremony at St. Phillips in Atlanta. For her, the first year or so after the accident was a painful blur. She, her husband, and new baby daughter moved to Madison, Wisconsin, while he worked on his Ph.D. in Political Science. When they first arrived in Madison, the young couple lived for six weeks in a tent while they awaited a house to rent. That, Linda remembers, was the beginning of a "new, simple, and manageable life. It was easy to sweep the tent and roll up the sleeping bags." Meanwhile, Reese married his high school sweetheart after his sophomore year at Georgia and upon graduation went to work for his Uncle Hicks at Lanier Business Products.

College-aged children like Reese were already in the process of severing home ties, and that made the transition somewhat easier. Steve Clay—whose biological father had also died in a plane crash—returned to Atlanta after his mother Sally Benson perished at Orly and his step-father died shortly thereafter. His friend David Black, then home on vacation from Washington and Lee, had lost his mother, Lydia, in the crash. David along with another friend met Steve at the airport and took him to his house with his father and younger brother Fred, then a student at Westminster. He remained there for the summer and several summers to come. The three "sort of became a fraternity," Steve remarked. "It gave me a place to be and a way to be back in Atlanta."

Another tragedy darkened Steve Clay's already dismal summer. The family had waited several weeks to tell his grandmother of her daughter's death because she was frail and had a serious heart condition. When they finally did reveal the sad news, the elderly lady collapsed and died. As he related the sequence of terrible events, Steve remarked wistfully: "One of the principal effects of the crash is that there are no unexpected tragedies that ever occur in my life. They're always expected." But being a strong survivor, he grew up fast and worked out a positive way to restructure his life. Upon his graduation from Yale, he married his girlfriend, Henny, and created a new family of his own.

Penny Armstrong, who had also lost her biological father when she was young, developed an inner sense of survival. After returning to Atlanta the day after her mother died at Orly, she spent the long month waiting for the return of Henrietta's remains. Then soon after the funeral, she resumed her studies at the Sorbonne and traveled through Europe with the Hollins group. When she graduated two years later, she contemplated graduate school, but decided instead to sign up to be a Pan Am stewardess. "I don't think I was the least bit conscious of the irony of this at the time," she said, "but it sort of sounds like getting back onto a horse." She isn't sure whether the crash had anything to do with her decision to fly all over the world in a 707 or not. "It might have been that I happened to speak French," she smiled, "and wanted to travel on somebody else's money and it was just that simple. Or it could be both. But I'd be darned if I would let something like that get me." The loss of her mother, Penny said, "made me real independent and real determined to take care of myself, to do what needed to be done and move on."

Others, who were young adults at the time, shared that attitude. "One of the hardest things at that age," said Reese Lanier, "was that I didn't have anybody to go ask things. His aunt Claudia "tried very hard," he said. "She bought me stationary. She taught me how to write my notes to the debutante party and accept with pleasure and regret." Nevertheless, he found it "a lot different than having parents to ask" and "I think it made us all extremely independent." His sister, Linda, echoed his sentiments. "There was something also about a burden of responsibility that I think we all felt very strongly."

Most of the children who lost their mothers did have the immediate security of remaining with their fathers in the same house. In most cases, the fathers eventually remarried and life settled into a new pattern, albeit the readjustment was difficult. That eventually happened in the Bevington family, but the immediate effect of the crash was devastating for both father and sons. As instructed, his friend had taken Milton Jr. (nine), Rickey (eight), and Peter (seven), to North Georgia. When Milton arrived there a day or so later, he told the boys about the deaths of their mother and grandmother without realizing they already suspected it. "We read it on the front page of the newspaper," Peter said. "It had a picture of the tail and we put two and two together." After things settled down, life went on. "Obviously we missed our mother," Peter commented, "but he [Milton] just kept the family going. We weren't rejected or isolated or anything else."

Before grief counseling became commonplace after a tragedy, well-intended adults made unconscious mistakes. Tom Little hated grown-ups comforting him by saying: "I know how you feel." He was certain that "they didn't know, they couldn't have known." Inge Hill remembers people telling him: "This is God's will, this is God's plan." That, of course, made him think: "What did I do to deserve this." If "God is all knowing and all powerful, He could have come up with a better plan." But as an adult, Inge realized that "a lot of well-meaning people didn't know how to cope with it themselves," and thus "they would say the wrong thing" to children.

Perhaps the most damaging advice given to children, who lost their mothers or both parents, was telling them to "carry on with their lives" as if nothing had happened. Walt Crimm remembered people acting like his parents never existed. "Things were sort of removed from the house," he said. "There was a sort of purging." Inge Hill agreed: "It wasn't as if your mother had died, it was as if you never had a mother." His sister, Lee Hill Beck, remembered that her friends thought it was strange that no one in her household ever referred to their mother. "You never talked about it, you never even mentioned their name for fear that you as a child might upset the adults," commented Pat Little Reynolds. Children were never taken to funerals, she said. "It was not the accepted thing. I never went to my grandparents' funeral or aunts' and uncles'. So the first funeral I attended was my parents' and that was quite a jolt because I had never done it before."

This type of adult shielding often produced amazingly similar dreams. Several of the younger children dreamt that their parents had amnesia as a result of the crash and were really alive and wandering around somewhere unable to find their families. Inge Hill said he dreamt of himself and his mother having a joyous reunion, and he would wake up all excited, only to face reality and "relive the whole thing."

Columnist, Doris Lockerman, who had experienced the death of her own mother when she was young, realized how difficult it was for children to cope with the loss of parents. "People take grief differently," she said. Some wanted "to be talked to and really wanted to remember. But others hated people talking to them." A few months after the crash, she attempted to write a follow-up on the surviving children but was discouraged from pursuing it. "The people who had taken them as foster parents did not want them to be disturbed by stirring up unhappy memories," she said, and it made her realize that she was perceived as intruding rather than comforting.

A consolation for the children of Anne Merritt—Bill (eighteen), Anne (fifteen), and Marti (ten)—was that their mother always said that "if she could choose a way to die," she wanted it to be on a return trip from Europe, which meant that she was dying happy. Not only had Anne Merritt's wish come true, but most of her friends perished as well. Her son Bill saw the crash as marking the "end of an entire social order" which coincided, he thinks, "with the end of the then-existing social order in Atlanta." For the lives of the Merritt children and that of their father, it surely marked a pivotal, if painful, transition.

Grief was palpable on the morning of June 4, when the executive committee of the Atlanta Art Association met in an emergency session. Chairman of the Board, James V. Carmichael—who had been in Washington when news of the crash broke—canceled his business trip and hurriedly returned home. "It's like an atomic bomb had hit Atlanta," Carmichael told reporters. "It has simply wiped out our basic support. These were the hard workers, the people we depended on." In addition to losing the association's president, Del Paige and his wife Winifred, three additional board members—Ruth McMillan, Raiford Ragsdale, and Sidney Wien—perished at Orly. Carmichael was mourning several personal losses as well. Randy Berry was one of his chief executives at Scripto; Elizabeth Blair, widow of his late law partner, was his next-door-neighbor; and Adelaide McDonald was his wife's cousin.

As the Art Association's executive committee met in the Members' Room on June 4, the local and national media gathered in the lobby. Inside closed doors, the board's leaders—many having lost family members and close friends—decided to make no decisive announcements. They agreed, however, to establish a memorial fund but were too upset to make any definite decision about how the money should be spent. They merely specified that their efforts would in no way conflict with the city's plans to build an art center in Piedmont Park. Following an executive committee meeting four days later, Carmichael announced that contributions in memory of the Orly victims would go toward building a new $1.5 million art school.

Having a specific focus for the memorial fundraising not only pleased the press—which ran major articles about the new school—but it proved to be the first step in implementing the recently approved Engelhardt report. About two-thirds of the money collected would go toward a new building; the remainder would provide scholarships for "deserving art students" and operating funds for the entire facility. After all of the trustees approved of channeling memorial contributions toward the newly christened Atlanta School of Art, Carmichael told the press that the entire association needed "a complete overhauling," and he compared the planned reorganization to the operation of a "well-run business." In short, there would be a visible shift from volunteer service to well-oiled professionalism. As a memorial to those many volunteers who perished at Orly, this pronouncement carried a ringing irony that would resound in the years to come.

When Eugene Patterson returned to Atlanta from Paris, he

took the roll of film he had found in the wreckage at Orly to the *Constitution* office for processing. It revealed an attractive young couple vacationing in Greece and someone at the paper identified them as Helen and Bill Cartledge. After ascertaining that information, Patterson called Frania Lee and arranged to deliver the photographs. "I found her to be most gracious in welcoming me into her home and thanking me for bringing her the pictures of her daughter," the editor recalled. "We had a very pleasant afternoon just talking about that trip and the terrible tragedy for Atlanta and for her personally having lost her daughter. I didn't stay too long, but long enough to know that she was a lady. I liked her."

At that time Frania Lee was already in the process of memorializing her daughter. In conjunction with the Women's Guild of Theatre Atlanta—to which Helen had devoted so much of her energies—Frania donated a substantial amount to build a new theater and acting school. Helen, who was only thirty-two when she died, had two principal goals: to provide a place where aspiring young actors and actresses could perform in Atlanta and to offer a school for their training. Frania Lee's generosity and the hard work of the Women's Guild members made that wish into a reality. The state-of-the art Theatre Atlanta on West Peachtree Street opened in 1968 and operated there for several years before experiencing financial problems. After Theatre Atlanta's departure, the resident theatre became Center Stage, which presented a creative variety of entertainment, supervised enthusiastically by Frania and her grandson, Ronny.

Other memorials were already springing up around the city. Within a week after the Air France crash, a then-unknown donor contributed a rose window to St. Phillips Episcopal Cathedral in memory of the victims. The church, which stands at the fork of Peachtree Road and Andrews Drive in Buckhead, was then undergoing a large expansion and renovation, so that certain projects were already earmarked for possible financing. That no doubt explains the rapid appearance of the memorial window, which fills the northern balcony wall over the apse. Beneath it hangs a tablet inscribed with the names of all those who perished at Orly. For many years, the donor remained anonymous and was simply noted as "a member of the Cathedral congregation who lost many devoted friends and fellow worshipers." Today, however, there is a small plaque identifying the benefactor as Isabelle Woolford Kennedy.

Milton Bevington worked through his grief by establishing a memorial fund to support research for children's diseases, which he called the Children's Medical Research Memorial fund. "My first thought was of our three sons," he told Doris Lockerman a week after the crash. "I saw those terrible flames leap into the air and was stricken with what it would mean to them to lose their mother and grandmother. Since then I have passed through shock, agony, dejection, and even self-pity and bitterness," he confided. "Now with this tide of kindness that has swept over me, I have come to a new feeling for others, a new sense of appreciation, a motivation to channel this great goodness of mankind to something constructive." His first step was to set up an organization to collect and dispense the funds; then he solicited the support of clergymen as well as people who lost relatives in the Orly crash. The public relations department of the Coca-Cola Company helped by donating a colorful brochure to advertise the project.

During the following year, Bevington was able to interest many people in his research fund, including one of the leading physicians at the Harvard Medical School. In behalf of his project, he spoke in Washington at a meeting of the General Federation of Women's Clubs, then one of the largest non-profit organizations in the world. Initially his goal was to establish either a children's research hospital, a research chair at a major medical school, or a scholarship fund for students specializing in childhood diseases. None of these objectives fully materialized. Yet with help from several families, he was able to raise around $6,000, which went toward researching emotional illnesses at the Child Behavior Research Center Unit of Boston's Massachusetts General Hospital. If the fund failed to meet its original long-term goals, it did make a contribution to medical research; and it provided Bevington with a positive means through which to convert his own sorrow into helping others.

Individual memorials to those lost at Orly appeared in surprising places. In Toronto, Canada, where Anne and Randolph Berry had lived for awhile, a new Ontario Crippled Children's Center was dedicated in their memory. Friends in Canada also donated the statue of a child that was placed at the Atlanta Cerebral Palsy Clinic, where Anne had devoted many hours as a dedicated volunteer. Every year during her lifetime, Anne's mother, Mrs. D.C. Black, went out to the clinic to place a wreath at the foot of the statue. The Atlanta Junior League, which lost thirteen members, donated an acoustical shell in their memory to the Atlanta Symphony. The Georgia and Atlanta Residence Lighting Forums dedicated a memorial fountain at the Georgia Power Company to Ruth Morris, who spent a better part of her life designing residential lighting.

Most memorial gifts, however, went to the Atlanta Art Association. James Carmichael's announcement of the new art school meant that donations coming from around the world would be funneled into that project. The drive received unexpected publicity in the national press, especially *Life* magazine, which ran a long article about the crash, featuring several of the victims and picturing works from the High Museum collection.

It was the first time any painting from the museum had been photographed in color, much less published. Thus when *Life* donated the slides to the museum, requests for copies poured into the association office. Suddenly, the floundering organization was receiving national and international attention, a spotlight it was totally unprepared to handle.

Nevertheless the director, Reginald Poland—with the help of his volunteer staff—answered each sympathy letter, telegram, and order for photographs. In each letter, he would insert a plug for supporting a new Atlanta College of Art. One of the more thoughtful gifts came from Louisville, Kentucky, where a local organization sold paintings and other art objects to raise money for the proposed Atlanta school. Poland was so touched by the gesture that he flew there at his own expense. Sales went well enough for Louisville to present the Atlanta Art Association a check for $1,250.

At the same time, an exhibition of paintings was taking place in the High Museum's "Browse, Borrow and Buy" gallery. Its purpose was to honor artists killed in the Orly crash. In addition to showing works by professional artists David Cogland, Doug Davis, and Helen Seydel, it included paintings by Betsy Bevington, Helen Cartledge, Mary Louise Perkins, Dolly Brooks, Adelaide McDonald, Nell Lanier, Puddin' Humphreys, Molly Bull, and Julia Jones.

These memorial fundraising efforts were so successful that within a few months of the tragedy, the Atlanta Art Association had collected an estimated $50,000 toward its $1.5 million goal. Now they were faced with the big question: where do we go from here?

Mayor Ivan Allen Jr., circa 1961
(Courtesy Atlanta History Center)

The J.M. High House (Old High Museum 1926–1966)
(Courtesy Atlanta History Center)

Thornton House at High Museum, early 1960s
(Restored under the direction of Tom and Charlotte Little)
(Courtesy Atlanta History Center)

Atlanta Art Association tour departing Atlanta, May 9, 1962
(Courtesy Mildred Seydell papers, Special Collections and Archives,
Robert W. Woodruff Library, Emory University)

Vasser Woolley Jr.
(Courtesy Mildred Seydell papers,
Special Collections and Archives, Robert
W. Woodruff Library, Emory University)

Henrietta Collier Armstrong
(later Ayer) and daughter Penny,
circa 1948
(Courtesy Penny Armstrong Hart)

Sykes and Carroll M. Young,
Venice, 1962
(Courtesy Carroll Young)

Mildred and Saul Gerson, circa 1960
(Courtesy Robert L. Gerson)

Tom and Charlotte Little photo
taken in booth in Atlanta on
the day of their departure for
Europe, May 9, 1962
(Courtesy Pat Little Reynolds)

Raiford Ragsdale, circa 1955
(Courtesy Jane Wellborn)

Ruby Stow, circa 1950
(Courtesy Jane Stow Greene)

Clementina MacPherson, 1950s
(Courtesy Lee Hill Beck)

Raiford Ragsdale, Lydia Black, Ruth McMillan, Lake Lucerne,
May 1962 *(Courtesy Jane Wellborn)*

David Black, Nancy Pegram, Bob Pegram, Lydia
Black, Atlanta Airport, May 9, 1962
(Courtesy Ann Pegram Harris)

Morris Brandon, Nancy Pegram, Martha Brandon at Atlanta
Airport awaiting departure, May 9, 1962
(Courtesy Ann Pegram Harris)

Tommy and Nell Lanier on his fiftieth birthday, Portofino, Italy,
May 1962 *(Courtesy J. Reese Lanier)*

Helen Seydel on her wedding day, 1935
(Courtesy Susan Seydel Cofer)

Lee MacPherson Virgin, 1950s
(Courtesy Frank Virgin)

Frances MacPherson Hill, 1958
(Courtesy Lee Hill Beck)

Julia Block (later Jones),
1930s
(Courtesy Baxter P. Jones)

Gladys Kaye, circa 1960
(Courtesy Audrey Goldstein)

Arnold Kaye, circa 1960
(Courtesy Audrey Goldstein)

Paul Barnett, 1950s
(Courtesy Guerry Barnett Russell)

Rosalind Williams, circa 1955
(Courtesy Linda W. Williams)

Ruby Martin Adair, circa 1960
(Courtesy J. Wesley Martin)

Harry and Mary Boon in
Holland, May 1962
(Courtesy Ann Boon Rhea)

Mary Ansley Howland, October, 1932, on her honeymoon trip to
Europe *(Courtesy Dr. W. Slocum Howland)*

Allee Tidmore, left, and Mildred Dilts, right, with tour group in Holland, May 1962 *(Courtesy Terresa Tidmore Turner)*

Atlanta Art Association tour group at Palais de Versailles, May 1962 *(Courtesy Jane Wellborn)*

Charles Baxter Jones Jr., 1952, the
year he ran for Congress
(Courtesy Baxter P. Jones

David Cogland with one of his paintings, circa 1961
(Courtesy Rosa Baskett)

Susan Coltrane and Lucy Candler, Oxford, England, May 1962
(Courtesy Atlanta History Center)

Winifred and Del Paige, Oxford, England, May 1962
(Courtesy Atlanta History Center)

Celebrating the arrival of Auguste Rodin's *L'Hombre* or *The Shade* at the Memorial Arts Center, October 1968. The French ambassador to the United States, Charles Lucet, presented the statue to the Atlanta Arts Alliance in memory of those who perished at Orly.
(Courtesy Robert W. Woodruff Arts Center)

PART IV

The Phoenix Rises

CHAPTER 14

✖ Building a Memorial

On May 22, 1962, a colorful brigade of musicians, dancers, actors, and Arts Festival officials stood in front of City Hall carrying baskets of petitions supporting the proposed cultural center in Piedmont Park. When tallied, the documents contained 35,637 signatures, an amount deemed sufficient to convince the bond commission that the park project should be included in the upcoming referendum.

The person most enthusiastic about the proposed center was Philip Weltner, chief advisor for Robert Woodruff's charitable foundation. He had been working hard to convince his boss to pledge $4 million anonymously, if the city would pay another $3 million, for preparing the park. While Weltner and Woodruff were debating the configuration and composition of the center, tragedy struck at Orly and overnight everything changed. Del

Paige—who was president of both the Atlanta Art Association and the city's Cultural Needs Committee—had died, obliterating the most forceful link between the park project and museum. Julia Jones and Raiford Ragsdale, trustees of both the symphony and museum, had also died at Orly, eliminating two more influential connections between the two ventures.

Weltner realized right away that the going would be tough. When Carmichael announced a fundraising drive for the new school less than a week after the crash, the educator wrote Woodruff in distress: "The papers today are carrying front page stories about Jimmy's plan to raise $1,500,000 for an Atlanta Memorial Art Institute," he said. "By going it alone the plan is bound adversely to affect our proposal to raise an even larger sum for the Community Center, whether his drive goes over the top or not."

Weltner was right. By the middle of July, the art school campaign had raised so much money that the momentum was impossible to stop. Carmichael's authority was strengthened when the trustees elected him to assume Paige's duties as president of the Art Association in addition to those he already possessed as board chairman. Although the $3 million earmarked for renovating Piedmont Park was only a small segment of $80 million bond referendum, the media played up the proposed cultural center because it had become so controversial.

Several factors were adversely affecting the park project. For one thing, members of the city's white power structure began adopting Weltner's view that it was an either-or proposition, and thus they split over whether to support their friend, Ivan Allen, or their business colleague, Jimmy Carmichael. In addition to this division within the city's commercial leadership, misconceptions were arising because Woodruff refused to allow his name to be connected to the promised $4 million grant. In some quarters, the "anonymous donor" was whispered to be African American millionaire Alonzo Herndon, a rumor that only exacerbated the already volatile racial atmosphere. For most white voters, use of tax dollars to fund any kind of public facility in a desegregated city park was anathema. Blacks were also skeptical, viewing the proposed cultural center as yet another white-dominated institution that would exclude them.

The lack of enthusiasm among the commercial leadership and the general population made defeat inevitable. In the election that August, voters overwhelmingly rejected the referendum, with the park project losing two-to-one. But on other fronts, things were changing during the autumn of '62. With the county-unit system no longer determining the results of local elections, Philip Welter's son Charles—a strong supporter of integration—defeated the deeply entrenched and ultraconservative James C. Davis to become Fifth District Congressman. So even though the Piedmont Park project failed ostensibly as a protest against desegregation, Atlanta was showing other signs of integrating African Americans into its society without major incidents.

The Piedmont Park cultural center may well have been another victim of the Orly crash. If Paige had lived, perhaps things would have been different. The gentle peacemaker with an influential role in both camps probably could have rallied the power structure behind the park center and brought members of the museum board along with him. But as it was, a group of hard-knuckled businessmen were filling the void left by the deaths of so many enthusiastic volunteers. The crash also focused attention on the location of the trip's origin. The Atlanta Art Association—where many of those killed had donated their services or joined painting classes—seemed the obvious place to build a memorial.

The Engelhardt report, which Paige and others had endorsed before leaving for Europe, emphasized the importance of a new art school. Now the enterprise seemed destined to succeed.

While the Piedmont Park referendum was floundering, Carmichael was moving at full speed. The Association board enlisted Rich's president, Richard H. Rich, to chair its fundraising drive and formed a team of leading businessmen to reassess the Art Association's mission. As civic leaders they realized that the symphony needed a new home, and many were enticed by the idea of bringing all of the arts under one umbrella. At the end of 1962, Dr. Wilhelmus Bryan, one of the three men who had conducted the Engelhardt study, became the new Art Association Director, and in that job served as an overseer for both the school and museum. A courtly, flamboyant individual, Bryan was an articulate showman with a worldly and sophisticated manner that conveyed an image of bravado and confidence. He appeared to be the perfect transitional figure.

Atlantans, who had previously ignored the arts, were beginning to take notice. In February 1963, the French government loaned the United States three famous paintings from its Louvre Museum in memory of those killed. But due to questionable security at the Atlanta Art Association (and Jackie Kennedy's wish to have one of the French paintings exhibited in Washington), Leonardo da Vinci's *Mona Lisa,* was shown only at the National Gallery. However, James A. McNeill Whistler's *Study in Grey and Black* (better known as "Whistler's Mother") and Georges de la Tour's *La Madeleine de la Veilleuse* (or *Mary Magdalene with a Night Light)* were shown in Atlanta. In the catalogue accompanying the two paintings, French Ambassador Hervé Alphand described Whistler's mother as a "great southern lady," who represents the "mysterious element of the American spirit." An estimated 100,000 people visited the museum to view the paintings and the national media was on the spot to cover the event on the *Today* show.

In March of '63, the Art Association hired Gudmund Vigtel to take Poland's place as director of the High Museum. "Vig," as everyone called him, was a native Norwegian, who came to the United States in the late 1940s to attend Piedmont College in Demorest, Georgia, on a Rotary scholarship. After spending the required time in the small mountain community, he transferred to the Atlanta Art Institute. Subsequently, he pursued his studies in art and art history, eventually becoming an assistant director of the Corcoran Gallery in Washington. When Carmichael approached Vigtel with the prospect of coming back to Atlanta to establish the High Museum as a more professional museum, the handsome and energetic Norwegian readily accepted the challenge.

And a challenge it was. When he arrived, Vigtel found the permanent collection included numerous works of dubious attribution, three disjointed buildings, and an arcane administrative setup. He joked later that he could fit the entire museum staff into a Volkswagen, because it then consisted of only five people, including himself. But he moved fast, hired qualified assistants, and began removing the questionable works and replacing them with those of higher quality. While increasing his staff, Vigtel still utilized volunteers. But instead of allowing them free reign to use the museum as a surrogate social club, he steered them into functional roles that would enhance his goals. Vigtel's housecleaning and his steps toward placing the institution on a professional footing were consequences of the Orly crash. Although implementation of the Engelhardt report eventually would have prompted such changes, they now seemed to move more rapidly with increased attention directed toward the Art Association.

The art school was also moving toward professionalism.

Around the time that Vigtel arrived, Joel Reeves—an amiable artist and faculty member for more than a decade—assumed the new title of school dean. Guthrie Foster, whose role in reorganizing the institution and gaining accreditation were invaluable, became Director of Admissions. Meanwhile, the art school was waiting anxiously to find out when, how, and whether the proposed new building would materialize.

A few days after the Piedmont Park project failed, Philip Weltner told his boss that they should seek an alternative location for the cultural center. In early 1963, they briefly considered a slum district being cleared for urban renewal, southeast of downtown on the edge of the interstate. That plan fizzled, however, when a coalition of businessmen and civic leaders purchased the property for a new baseball stadium. This turn of events caused the Woodruff Foundation to consider combining forces with the Art Association. If they could acquire enough land adjacent to the museum and school, then they could construct their cultural center on the corner of Peachtree and Fifteenth Streets.

One major sticking point was a verbal battle between Philip Weltner and James V. Carmichael. In a nutshell, Weltner strongly opposed including the art school in the conglomerate, and Carmichael—although enticed by Woodruff's $4 million pledge—was equally as determined to carry through the project for which he had already collected so many memorial contributions. "Jimmy is dead set to do his arts school," Weltner complained to Woodruff in June '63, "and is stone deaf to a total perspective embracing all the arts." After receiving this memo, Woodruff apparently called Carmichael and made a date for lunch. Woodruff would have to include the school and museum in his proposed cultural center if he wanted to build it on the Peachtree property.

With a green light from the Woodruff Foundation, preliminary planning could begin. A team of businessmen, headed by Richard Rich, formed a "Policy and Planning Committee." In July 1963, Carmichael announced that a new parent organization, known as the Atlanta Arts Alliance, would be replacing the existing Art Association, and within the next few months, the original planning committee expanded to include more businessmen along with representatives of the symphony, theatre, and ballet. In short, a year after the crash, the old Art Association had been transformed from a casual mélange of women volunteers into a highly businesslike enterprise run by bankers and corporate executives.

One obstacle to the Arts Alliance plan was purchasing the land that was locked into the wills of Hattie High and Edgar P. McBurney. After several conversations with lawyers, the High heirs agreed to relinquish the property as long as the museum bore the family name. Hence the title "Art Association" was formally dropped, and the building officially became known as the High Museum. The McBurney estate was also eventually persuaded to allow the Arts Alliance to tear down the old McBurney home, as long as the new museum would feature decorative arts prominently. Thornton House—the project that Charlotte and Tom Little had nursed into fruition--also needed to be moved from the property. Despite several loudly-voiced protests, the Arts Alliance struck a deal with Stone Mountain Park to move the antebellum building onto its property.

Perhaps the greatest obstruction to the new center came from the Women's Committee that wanted to retain its Coach House. Seeing the writing on the wall, they began making contingency plans. Twelve women, calling themselves the "Dirty Dozen," each pledged $10,000 to form the Forward Arts Foundation dedicated to supporting the arts in Atlanta. While these women were searching for a place to center their activities, the mayor's wife, Louise Allen, was in the process of arranging for the Atlanta Historical Society to move to the twenty-six acre former estate of her uncle, Edward Inman. In that wooded Buckhead location, the Historical Society built a new facility for exhibition and research while turning the Inman's 1920s mansion into a house-museum, now know as the Swan House. In back was an old garage that made a perfect home for the Coach House tea-room and gift shop.

In March 1964, the Woodruff Foundation agreed to pledge $4 million toward the new building, but only if the Arts Alliance would accept its conditions. Woodruff did not want his name attached to the promised gift; his donation hinged on collecting $3 million in matching funds; and he asked to review the architectural plans. With the "anonymous donation" finally secured, the Arts Alliance began seeking matching funds. Toward that end, the planning committee hired local fundraisers Claude Grizzard and Be Haas to orchestrate the campaign and published an elaborate brochure explaining the project. The initial efforts to raise money were so successful that the projected goal was increased to $7 million, the additional amount earmarked to cover operating costs. To kickoff the drive, the President's wife, Lady Bird Johnson, came to Atlanta in May '64 to unveil a model of the center prepared by the firm of Toombs, Amisano, and Wells.

Joseph Amisano, the architect in charge of the project, had designed a simple rectangular structure that would enclose the existing museum building at the front, adding a third floor for more exhibition space and a fourth floor for the art school. On the rear of the entrance level would be a 1,848-seat symphony hall and an 868-seat theatre, both served by a spacious galleria. When Woodruff exercised his right of reviewing the plan, he disapproved. It was far too stark for his taste and he insisted upon softening the façade with a row of columns. Since no one could argue with the man who controlled the purse strings, Amisano reluctantly added a lighted colonnade.

Costs for the new building exceeded the original estimate, and Woodruff agreed to add another $2.5 million if the Alliance would match half of his gift. A grass-roots campaign solicited individuals and small businesses, even targeting school children in what became known as "Operation Button Week." Ultimately, the community raised an estimated $600,000 and added $60,450 more collected from a concert on April 1, 1965, starring Jack Benny as guest violin soloist. The drive finally reached its goal in May 1966, after the Callaway Foundation pledged $1 million. The Atlanta Arts Alliance was finally able to break ground for the Memorial Arts Center on June 3, 1966, the fourth anniversary of the Orly crash.

The arts merger had already produced two casualties. Symphony director, Henry Sopkin—who had transformed the orchestra from amateur to professional—was politely but firmly persuaded to retire. Officials of the Alliance had already been in Cleveland negotiating with Robert Shaw in hopes that he would come to Atlanta. When Vigtel took charge of the High Museum and Joel Reeves stepped in to lead the art school, Wilhelmus Bryan's role was greatly diminished. When Rich, Carmichael, and other businessmen assumed management of the parent organization, Bryan became an unnecessary obstacle, and he was dismissed.

As the new Memorial Art Center was rising on the corner of Peachtree and Fifteenth Streets, relatives of those being memorialized were preparing to sue Air France. The case reached a federal panel of judges on September 16, 1963, when pretrial hearings began in Atlanta. At this point, thirty-three different plaintiffs had joined the litigation, each presenting similarly-worded cases that totaled claims for $18 million in damages. The lead attorney coordinating all the individual cases was William Schroder, a well-respected Atlanta attorney. Assisting him was the lawyer, Bates Block—Julia Jones's brother and guardian of the three Jones children—serving as lead plaintiff; and aiding the team was New York attorney Lee Kreindler, an aviation expert. Air France employed E. Smythe Gambrell, a colorful Atlanta lawyer, to argue its case.

The major issue confronting the court at that juncture was whether or not to limit the amount paid each family to $8,291, a cap on liabilities mandated by the pre-World War II Warsaw Convention. Before the hearings, Gambrell had begun offering individual families the amount allowed by the treaty if they would agree not to join the suit. Several of those contacted accepted the payment, while others were so disgusted with the process, they refused to apply for any compensation. No payment, they said, would make up for the loss of their loved ones. Others joned in the litigation.

A month of legal squabbling over procedural matters clouded the hearings, but the lawyers finally reached a compromise. U.S. District Judge Lewis R. Morgan agreed to hear the case which was scheduled to begin in November. By then three more families had joined the litigation, raising the amount sought to $20 million. Their claims, however, would be moot if they could not overcome the restriction imposed by the Warsaw Convention which the United States endorsed in 1934. And the only way that could be accomplished was to prove the airline guilty of "willful misconduct." That proof would come when the team of international investigators issued its report.

Meanwhile, lawyers for the plaintiffs were preparing their briefs, which they brought before Judge Morgan in May 1964. By then forty-three families had joined the suit, bringing the total amount sought to $26 million. After hearing arguments for both sides, Morgan upheld the restrictions imposed by the Warsaw Convention, awaiting word of Air France's guilt. If that were to occur, the judge said, then each case would go before a jury to determine the amount to be awarded. For the next three years the case languished in the judiciary system, until at last the Fifth District Circuit Court in New Orleans upheld Judge Morgan's opinion, a decision echoed by the U.S. Supreme Court. At that point a few of the plaintiffs settled for $8,291 in order to have closure, but the case was far from over.

In February 1965, the International Civil Aviation Organization (ICAO) issued its report on the crash. Although a photographic flight-recorder had been pulled from the wrecked tail, it revealed little, and at a time before airplanes were equipped with black boxes to record cockpit conversations, ascertaining the actual cause was purely speculative. Nevertheless, the ICAO reported that the problem seemed to have been in the trim tabs. The board of experts concluded "that an out-of-trim configuration existed and jamming of the trim mechanism prevented the pilot from correcting it during take-off." That malfunction could have been a flaw in the Boeing 707, which had previous problems with those tabs. But the report significantly added that Hoche could have flown the craft anyway. Tests held during the investigating process proved that the pilot "could have overcome the load on the control column and completed the take-off without endangering the continuation of the flight, even in the absence of any possibility of altering the trim."

The international investigators' report spelled triumph for the plaintiffs in the litigation against Air France. It clearly accused the airline of "willful misconduct," by stating that a combination of mechanical failure and pilot error caused the crash. After several more years of negotiations and a trip to France, William

Schroder and his team quietly settled out of court for $5.2 million. Although it was less than they had hoped to obtain, the amount paid by Air France turned out to be the largest settlement ever made up to that time for a single airplane crash. Those families that stuck with the case until its conclusion received proportionate pieces of the pie in separate agreements that averaged about $84,000 apiece. Sadly, Schroder never saw the completion of his hard work, because he died while the settlements were still pending.

The government of France attempted to make amends for its aviation blunder by rewarding Atlanta with a major sculpture for the new Memorial Arts Center. When it opened in October 1968, the French Ambassador to the United States, Charles Lucet, presented Auguste Rodin's *L'Ombre,* or *The Shade,* to the city. The dramatic statue, first conceived in 1880, is a bronze cast of a figure atop the sculptor's *Gates of Hell,* an enormous door originally designed for Paris's Museum of Decorative Arts. The Rodin sculpture was the icing on what turned out to be a very controversial cake.

When all the bills came in, the Memorial Arts Center's costs topped $13 million. Most of those funds went for construction of the 296,750-square-foot rectangular box that housed the museum, school, symphony hall, and two theatres (a larger one on the main floor and a small studio theatre in the basement). The new multi-purpose center was in keeping with a trend that reached its peak during the 1960s, its two most famous examples being Lincoln Center in New York and the Kennedy Center in Washington.

Although the Memorial Arts Center is a smaller version of those colossal undertakings, it is in many ways more ambitious. When it opened in 1968, it incorporated the city's *only* symphony, a conglomerate theatre company, the city's *only* comprehensive art museum, and the region's best-known independent art school—all under one roof. Typical of the chauvinistic spirit that has driven so many of the city's projects, the Memorial Arts Center was what *The New York Times* architectural critic, Ada Louise Huxtable, called "putting all of one's cultural eggs into one monumental basket." She criticized both the concept, which she saw as an ongoing financial drain, and the structure, which—like similar buildings in other cities—looked as if it had been designed by "a cultural center computer."

Despite such criticism, Woodruff (still listed as the "anonymous donor") toured the new facility and seemed pleased with what he had helped create. He remained quietly behind the scenes when the Memorial Arts Center opened with much fanfare on October 5, 1968. On the evening before the building made its public debut, Richard Rich hosted a black-tie gala for the trustees on the stage of the new Symphony Hall. George Goodwin and his wife Skip were there. She remembered that the "stage was transformed by a background of dark green velvet curtains, and tables were laid with fine china, silver and candelabra." After the dinner "served by white-gloved waiters," she remembers "looking out on the empty auditorium," knowing that she would never forget that "magical evening."

On the following afternoon a formal ceremony took place in the four-story tall galleria. Ambassador Lucet made a short speech when he unveiled *The Shade,* saying with a typical Gallic flair that the sculpture represented a "reconciliation of death and destiny." The museum subsequently placed the dramatic statue on the landing of a wide marble staircase accompanied by a plaque bearing the names of the 122 Air France passengers. That wall also carried an inscription that read: "Dedicated to all who truly believe the arts are a continuing effort of the human spirit to find meaning in existence, Orly, France, June 3, 1962."

For the grand opening of the center, each of its four separate components held an event. The High Museum staged an exhibition entitled "The Taste of Paris," displaying three centuries of paintings and drawings on loan from French museums. The Atlanta Symphony, now under the baton of its new director Robert Shaw, opened its '68-'69 season with selections from Wagner's *Die Meistersinger,* Aaron Copeland's *Canticle of Freedom,* and Beethoven's *Ninth Symphony.* A day earlier Joel Reeves, dean of the Atlanta School of Art, presided over a formal opening ceremony on the top floor of the building.

The new theatre presented perhaps the most spectacular—and in the long-run most disastrous—of the opening events. A few years earlier, several local groups had joined together to form the Atlanta Municipal Theatre (or AMT), under the direction of Christopher Manos. Because the AMT was an amalgam of a ballet, opera, children's theatre, and repertory theatre company, with an unwieldy administration and shaky financial footing, the Arts Alliance decided not to include it in its formal structure. Rather it leased out its new theatre to the group for one year with the possibility of annual renewals. Determined to showoff all of its accumulated talents for the grand opening, the AMT staged the American premier of *King Arthur,* an eighteenth century masque written by John Dryden and Henry Purcell. Although it gained widespread critical acclaim, the AMT greatly overspent its resources and was forced to declare bankruptcy. Since the business-oriented trustees of the Arts Alliance had no formal obligation to bail Manos out, they terminated their affiliation with him.

Therefore, three months after its formal dedication, the Memorial Center had an empty theatre. To avoid having the theatrical group's collapse jeopardize the entire center, the board hastily formed its own performing troupe, naming public-relations expert George Goodwin—a founding board member and a former chairman of Theatre Atlanta—to be an Alliance vice-chairman in charge of the project. In early 1969, a temporary company, directed by AMT's artistic director Michael Howard, produced four plays. The success of those productions won Howard a contract to form the Alliance Theatre, which eventually gained equal status in the Arts Alliance with the museum, art school, and symphony.

The opening of the Memorial Arts Center in October 1968—six months after Martin Luther King Jr.'s funeral cortege wound its mournful way from the Georgia State Capitol to Atlanta University—marked both an end and a beginning. Atlantans had slowly integrated all public facilities with no major incidents, even remaining calm in the wake of Dr. King's assassination, when riots were destroying other American cities. Mixed audiences attended concerts and plays at the new Arts Center, and African Americans were elected to sit on the boards of its different components. By 1968, Atlanta was on the move, leaving behind the Orly crash, which remained alive forever with those mourning personal losses.

CHAPTER 15

Changed Lives, Changed City

*f*or those who lost close relatives in the crash of 1962, the shadow of Orly has never gone away. Almost forty years later, descendants of those killed say their adult behavior has been irrevocably shaped by the tragedy. Several people commented that the loss of one or both parents ultimately gave them strength when facing adversity. But that lesson was not without a downside. "It gives you a better perspective on things," said Inge Hill. "When hardships happen, which they do to everybody, you think OK this is bad but we can deal with it."

Several others commented that experiencing those hardships as youngsters influenced the way they overprotected their own children. Fred Black, who was in high school when his mother Lydia died, said that as a single parent raising a son he never parts with his boy without saying he loves him. And he expects his son to "say it back because I might not ever see him again." For others, the experience of losing parents made them determined to teach their own offspring independence. "I made my children self-sufficient from a very early age," said Pat Little Reynolds, "in case I'm not there to finish the job."

For the many men who lost their wives at Orly, recovery was slow and often painful. Fred Black said that although David Black Sr. remarried and brought three step-sisters into the family, his father never completely recovered from the crash. It "really shut him down for the rest of his life," Fred commented. Three years after the crash, Milton Bevington married Paula Lawton, a young Atlanta lawyer, and within the next decade or so, they gave his boys four half-brothers and a half-sister. Several of the other widowers tried remarriage but found it didn't work.

Those without families in Atlanta also had a difficult time. Paul Barnett's wife, Olive, had no blood relative living anywhere near. At the time of the crash, her daughter, Guerry, was in Memphis and her son, Paul, in Wilmington, Delaware, leaving only one of her husband's cousins to help her through the long wait for the return of her husband's body. For the next few years, Olive shuttled back and forth between her children who were moving frequently. Finally she returned to Atlanta, where she lived alone for the rest of her life.

Without fail, all descendents of those killed commented on how they missed having grandparents for their children. Harry Boon's son was asked in school: if you could spend one day with any person living or dead, real or fictional, who would you choose? The boy replied that he would like to spend the day fishing with the grandfather he never knew. Ann Cantey Paine commented: "I would have loved watching Daddy tell his boyhood stories. . . . There are parts of my children's lives which are permanently altered by the absence of this vital extended family."

"My three children never knew their aunt" wrote Gregg Loomis whose sister, Louise, died in the crash. "I lost my closest buddy and the world is poorer thereby." Gregg and numerous others gradually readjusted and started life anew. Children grew up, attended college, married, pursued careers, and life went on. Several who lost parents at Orly remained determined to preserve their memories. Ann Cantey Payne says the tragedy turned her into the chronicler with the obligation to tell her own grandchildren stories about her parents. "I sometimes feel that I've built my family traditions starting from scratch," she commented, "because I know how important and how eternal the memories become over time." Clement Virgin Durkes expressed similar feelings: "I still have a very strong sense of heredity and my place in the long line of strong, intelligent, lovingly happy women who were my ancestors."

For all children whose parents died at Orly, the crash marked a watershed in their lives that strongly affected their relationships with others, especially spouses. Some marriages—like those of Steve Clay, Penny Armstrong Hart, Bob and Micheline Gerson, Tom Little and his sister Pat Little Reynolds—have survived for decades, many of them admitting that the loss of their parent or parents drew them closer together. Others say the crash led to an eventual divorce. "I remember that my first thought on hearing the news of my parents' deaths," Carroll Young said, "was now I'm on my own," and even in her grief she realized it was "a kind of liberation." Having dropped out of Vanderbilt to marry at age nineteen, she became gradually aware that she had been leading her life merely to fulfill "the conventional expectations" of her parents.

After her divorce in 1973, Carroll returned to Vanderbilt, earned a bachelors and a masters degree in nursing and a Ph.D. in clinical psychology. In her career, she worked first as a medical and psychiatric hospital staff nurse, then as a staff psychologist at the Nashville V.A. Hospital, and currently as a psychologist in private practice. Her specialty is treating people who have experienced trauma. Carroll's own traumatic experience led her to settle with a mate whose only social aspirations are helping others face difficult situations. She feels that the Orly crash heightened her "professional interest in the construction of meaning," and hopes that her personal quest to make her own life more meaningful has helped to instill meaning into the lives of others.

Marti Merritt also acknowledges that the loss of her mother at an early age shaped her later decision to enter the field of psychology and counsel children. Because of his parents' death, Sam Patz went to live with his ophthalmologist uncle who helped him develop an interest in medicine. He combined his exposure to the medical world with his longtime love of science and became a research physicist in Magnetic Resonance Imaging (MRI) at Harvard Medical School.

Sam's sister, Sarah Anne, pursued modern dance as a release for the "internal sadness and silence" that has haunted her ever since her parents' death. She received a masters degree in dance therapy, worked as the director of a dance company, and now teaches "Movement Arts" at Washington University in St. Louis. Her brother, Harry, said that after spending over twenty years being angry at the world for taking away his parents, he began to channel his hostility into helping others. At first, he volunteered in emergency response agencies as a firefighter, medic, and rescuer. Now he works in contingency planning, emergency preparedness, and emergency response, a much needed specialty in a world threatened by terrorist attacks. But one vestige from his youthful brush with tragedy remains. Although Harry Patz gets great satisfaction from his job, he prefers not to work with air crashes.

Most relatives of those killed agree that flying has been difficult, even though they continue to do it. "I have never taken off in an airplane when I didn't think there's a good chance this plane is going to crash," said Carroll Young. She has good reason to think that. In 1995, her youngest son was flying a small plane which crashed injuring him and killing his wife. Carroll and many of the other descendants of those on the Air France jet hold hands with spouses or other loved ones every time their plane takes off.

Reverberations from the tragedy extended beyond the families of those lost. Françoise Authie, one of the two stewardess miraculously blown out of the plane's tail, told reporters in 1972 that she stopped flying immediately after the crash and has never boarded another plane. Air France said that her colleague, Jacqueline Gillet, suffered a complete "nervous breakdown" as a result of being in the accident and would not talk to reporters.

Frania Lee, whose daughter Helen Cartledge died at Orly, did have a rewarding moment. In 1975, a year after the death of H.L. Hunt, she filed suit for her share of the billionaire's estate, which was being divided among his other two families. The case came to trial in Shreveport, Louisiana in 1978. After five days of testimony before a six-judge panel—during which Frania, appeared often on the witness stand—attorneys for the Hunts realized their case was weak and tried to settle out of court. Frania agreed to their terms and ultimately received $7.5 million. A photograph on the front page of the *Atlanta Constitution* showed her triumphantly leaving the courtroom with her grandson, Ronny, then age nineteen.

Other personal postscripts illustrate the persistent echoes of the disaster. When Gregg Loomis and his wife were in Venice in 1995, they spent a rainy day looking at Venetian glass. When one shopkeeper learned they were from Atlanta "he produced a huge leather-bound ledger in which the United States was subdivided by city. Under Atlanta, in Louise's handwriting, was her name and address." Amazed but saddened, Gregg realized that he had happened into the place where his sister had purchased the glasses that arrived after her death. Fred Black used his share of the Air France settlement to travel through Europe by motorcycle. One of his stops was the town of Villeneuve-le-Roi on the edge of Orly airport. He had perhaps hoped to learn something more about the crash, but as he walked around the edge of the airfield, he became aware that there was nothing there other than his own haunting memories.

In Atlanta, the phoenix was more than an abstract symbol, it was a mandate. Rising from the ashes signified not only rebuilding and recovery, but accelerated change. The Forward Atlanta campaign of the 1960s had been so successful that Atlanta popped out in all directions. Frederick Allen described it best. The city, he wrote in *Atlanta Rising,* was like "a teenager who gradually outgrew the clothes of childhood and got a new wardrobe, only to experience a sudden, secondary growth spurt that necessitated *another* complete change." Atlanta seemed to outgrow everything overnight: its boundaries, its roads, its sports facilities, its office buildings, and even its "new, modern" airport, which after less than twenty years after its opening was torn down and replaced with a newer, more modern hi-tech terminal. The phoenix was being transformed into a behemoth.

Atlanta didn't just rise from the ashes of Orly, it soared, leaving in its wake little public memory of the 122 artists, art lovers, business executives, housewives, lawyers, and doctors who died. Even the arts center, built ostensibly as a memorial to those killed, was reconfigured in the growth spurt. The new High Museum of 1968 soon felt cramped and in 1983 moved next door into a gleaming white structure designed by Richard Meier and partially financed by the no-longer-anonymous donor, Robert Woodruff. A year earlier, the Arts Alliance honored its ninety-three-year old benefactor who had poured $28 million into the institution by renaming it "The Robert W. Woodruff Arts Center." The original building kept the name "Memorial" in its title, but few paid attention to that. From that point on, everyone called the entire place the Woodruff Center.

Obliteration of the original inspiration for the center became controversial for a brief time in the early '80s, when *The Shade* mysteriously disappeared from its perch on the landing. After the new museum opened, it re-emerged on the third floor of the Meier building next to other pieces of sculpture. Granted Rodin's statue was more notable than any others in the High Museum's collection, but that was beside the point. It had been given by France as a memorial and was thus more appropriately displayed beside the names of those who died. Yet Atlanta's amnesia was so complete, it took several years for anyone other than relatives of the Orly victims to notice it was gone. Finally in 1987, its location captured the attention of the media, thus initiating a tug-of-war between Vigtel and Alliance authorities.

Following several months of haggling, *The Shade* returned to its original location with a new plaque, this time giving the women distinction by including their given and maiden names instead of listing them only as "Mrs. . . ." It was a sign of the changing times. Eight years later, *The Shade* was moved again. When the original Memorial Arts Center building was renovated in the mid '90s, the Rodin sculpture was moved to the front lawn, facing the traffic on Peachtree. Behind it is a low, black granite wall bearing the names of the people killed at Orly. Although bird droppings and beer cans sometime litter the site, most people agree it is a dramatic, if inaccessible, memorial. Several of the descendants expressed positive feelings, saying they thought *The Shade* was fitting commemoration of their lost loved ones. "To a large extent, the trip was about French art," commented Bill Merritt. "To me art is the only possible response to tragedy." Many of these same relatives feel disappointed, however, because most visitors to the High Museum never see the monument, and those who happen upon it know little about the tragedy that led France to donate it in 1962.

As one of the city's major attractions, the Woodruff Center is so successful that, like all of Atlanta, it is outgrowing its "clothes." The High Museum is constructing a major large addition, and the symphony is building a new hall, separate from, but nearby its present location. The school now known as the Atlanta College of Art boasts of being the only accredited four-year art college in Georgia. After taking over the space vacated by the High Museum in the early '80s, the ACA has 425 full-time students, 23 permanent faculty members, and an array of visiting artists and teachers. The Alliance Theatre has managed to survive several internecine struggles and continues to woo audiences to its productions on both the main stage and smaller Hertz stage in the basement. Despite the fact that the conglomerate has a clear monopoly of the arts in Atlanta, nobody has dared challenge it. Like the city that cheers it along, the Woodruff Center is brash, ambitious, and aggressive.

Del Paige, Ruth McMillan, Sidney Wien, Raiford Ragsdale, Julia Jones, Lydia Black, and all those active volunteers would be amazed to see what evolved out of the Atlanta Art Association. Now entirely slick and professional, no vestiges remain of the casual and often disorganized place they left in 1962. The five separate boards that govern the four components and parent organization are composed largely of business executives, who serve as a civic duty and only a handful have any real commitment to the arts. However, the current staff of the Woodruff Arts

Center has become increasingly conscientious about its mission to memorialize individuals lost in 1962. On the twentieth and thirtieth anniversaries of the Orly crash, it held ceremonies to commemorate the event; in October 2000, it hosted a meeting for relatives of the Orly victims; and a year later used its facilities to preview the television documentary about the crash.

In addition to the arts center, which sprang more-or-less from the ashes of Orly, the crash still leaves its legacy in the city. Baxter P. Jones, who lost his parents when he was five, is now an Atlanta attorney. He feels that the crash depleted Atlanta's arts leadership by removing what Ivan Allen called "the backbone of Atlanta's cultural society." And although Jones admits he "is not objective on the subject," he feels that "the city's arts community suffered a great loss" when the Air France jet crashed, and that absence of dedicated volunteers "accounts for much of the neglect we have been lamenting recently in newspaper articles and other forums." Several other relatives of those lost agree that the deaths of so many devotees of the arts left a void that has never been filled.

Unquestionably, many of the 106 Atlantans on the Art Association tour would have remained involved in the city's cultural life had they lived. But how many of them would have made a significant difference in a society growing as rapidly as Atlanta's? Perhaps only less than a third (or about 34 people) would have been involved at all. Artists like David Cogland, Doug Davis, and Helen Seydel surely would have contributed individually through their own talents that were obliterated far too soon. And Del Paige, Raiford Ragsdale, Julia Jones, Lydia Black, and a few other ardent volunteers would have shared their ideas with boards and other decision-making operations. The Atlantans who toured Europe in 1962 would have made an effort to involve their children in the arts of Atlanta, their ideas and experiences providing a stronger direction to those whose lives they touched.

Businesses that lost their chief executives had great difficulty recovering the damage done to their corporate structure and legal, architectural, and medical practices suffered similar devastating blows. Aubrey Morris said that the crash at Orly took Atlanta's "soul" and it never recovered. He explained that as the city grew, people with deep roots in its founding and early progress were no longer around to build and shape developments with dignity and deep commitment. And those who replaced them, regardless of race, had no longstanding ties with promoting Atlanta's interests.

The crash at Orly occurred at a pivotal moment when Atlanta and the nation were on the verge of dramatic social transformations. It is difficult to compare the small-town cultural atmosphere of '62 with the fast-paced and strident scene that evolved over the next forty years. Then there were dedicated volunteers, donating their time in hopes of holding together a poorly-funded museum, symphony, and school. Working alongside them were other teams struggling to save the symphony and other aspiring performing arts organizations. By the late '60s, the clique of prominent families that guided the city and its culture was fast being replaced. City Hall is a case in point. Ivan Allen, who had roots in the old Atlanta power structure, was followed by his Jewish vice-mayor, Sam Massell, who was the last white man to occupy the mayor's office. It might be convenient to credit the Orly crash with Atlanta's lost "soul," but because it happened when the entire country was undergoing tremendous changes, the tragedy in France formed a symbolic time marker.

Just think about it. The people who died at Orly never knew about the assassinations of President John F. Kennedy, his brother Robert, or Martin Luther King Jr. They had little, if any, knowledge of the Vietnam War. They never knew that a fellow Georgian would be President of the United States. They never saw the end of segregation and the free intermingling of whites and blacks (whom they still called "Negroes," if they were polite). They never knew that American men walked on the moon. And they never saw the word "terrorist" applied to activities within the nation's borders.

They never heard of the Beatles, the Grateful Dead, or Elton John. They never watched the Atlanta Braves play baseball. They had no knowledge of the Atlanta Falcons or Atlanta Hawks. Music came from long-playing records, not cassette tapes or compact discs. They wrote letters by hand or on typewriters. No one could imagine a personal computer much less a laptop. Nor could they possibly conceive of the Internet or email. Cell phones were only in comic strips.

Time for them froze at that airport on the edge of Paris in early June 1962. They were all happy and relaxed after three wonderful weeks of vacation. The city they left behind was forever bathed in magnolia blossoms and visiting Metropolitan Opera stars. Their last memories were of blooming horse chestnut trees, marvelous French food, and great European masterpieces. They never suffered. It was the individual families and friends who experienced the depth of loss and gradual recovery in a city and a world spinning rapidly. The tragic end of the Atlanta Art Association tour marked a symbolic finale to a slower-paced age. The term "Southern belle" still represented a living person, not a character in a novel; women and minorities knew their "places" in the complex social hierarchy. Perhaps significantly, sometime in 1962, Atlanta's Frances Virginia Tearoom served its last fried chicken and frozen-fruit salad, poured its last iced tea, and quietly closed its doors forever.

Notes

Published Sources

Chapter One: Lea Agnew and David Hughes Duke, "History of the Woodruff Arts Center," *Atlanta History* 38 (Spring-Summer, 1994), 32, 34, 48-52; 61-63; Franklin M. Garrett, *Atlanta and Environs: A Chronicle of Its People and Events* 3 (Athens, GA, 1954), 375, 558; *Atlanta Journal [AJ]* and *Atlanta Constitution [AC]*, Feb. 4, Apr. 6, June 3-5, 1962; Margaret Turner, *Atlanta Journal and Constitution [AJC]*, Feb. 18, 1962; Emma Edmunds, *AJC,* Sept. 3, 1981.

Chapter Two: Frederick Allen, *Atlanta Rising: The Invention of an International City, 1946-1996* (Atlanta, GA, 1996), 20-111; Taylor Branch, *Parting of the Waters: America in the King Years, 1954-1963* (New York, NY, 1988), 266-69; Harold Martin, *Atlanta and Environs: A Chronicle of Its People and Events,* 3 (Atlanta, Athens and London, Athens, GA, 1987), 3-311; Melissa Faye Greene, *The Temple Bombing* (Reading, MA, 1996); Garrett, *Atlanta and Environs,* 2: 831-833, 837-852; Sara Mitchell Parsons, *From Southern Wrongs to Civil Rights: The Memoir of a White Civil Rights Activist* (Tuscaloosa, AL, 2000), 40-50; Gary M.

Pomerantz, *Where Peachtree Meets Sweet Auburn* (New York, NY, 1996), 204-224, 251-275; Celestine Sibley, *AC,* May 19, 1953; Doris Lockerman, *AC,* Aug. 4, 1948, June 9, 1961, July 11, 1961; *AJ,* May 5, 1944, July 11, 1961; *AC,* Sept. 8, 1961.

Chapter Three: Ivan Allen Jr. and Paul Hemphill, *Mayor: Notes on the Sixties* (New York, NY, 1971), 64; Garrett, *Atlanta and Environs,* 1: 910, 2: 137-155, 235-36, 255, 531; *Citizens' History of Atlanta 1833-1902* (Atlanta, GA, 1902), 78; Susan Kessler Barnard, *Buckhead: A Place for All Time* (Athens, GA, 1996), 194-195; *Our First Century: The Robinson-Humphrey Company Story, 1894-1994,* (Atlanta, GA, 1994); Raleigh Bryans, *AJ,* Jan. 3, 1962; Yolande Gwin, *AJC,* Apr. 29, 1973; Eugene Patterson, *AC,* June 4, 1962; *AC,* Sept. 28, 1900; *AJ,* Oct. 30, 1961; *AJC,* Oct. 13, 1961.

Chapter Four: Lockerman, *AC,* May 9, 1962; Patterson, *AC,* June 5, 1962; Olive Ann Burns, *AJC,* Jan. 18, 1948; Margaret Turner, *AJC,* Dec. 2, 1951.

Chapter Five: Lee Agnew and Jo Ann Haden-Miller, *Atlanta and Its Lawyers: A Century of Vision: 1888-1988* (Atlanta, GA, 1988); Georgia Bar Assn., *A Memorial of Logan Edwin Bleckley* (Macon, GA, 1909, reprint 1982); Robert B. Semple Jr., "A City Shaken by Tragedy Rebounds in Spirit," *The National Observer,* August 20, 1962; Garrett, *Atlanta and Environs,* 3: 245, 256; Patterson, *AC,* June 5, 1962; *AJ* and *AC,* Apr. 15-29, 1962.

Chapter Six: *AJ* and *AC,* June 4, 1962; Kathryn Grayburn, *AC,* June 4, 1962.

Chapter Seven: F. Allen, *Atlanta Rising,* 116-118; Ardis Burst, *The Three Families of H. L. Hunt* (New York, NY, 1988); Stanley H. Brown, *H.L. Hunt* (Chicago, IL, 1976); Jack Strong, *AC,* May 9, 1962; Lockerman, *AC,* May 7, 1962; Ralph McGill, "A Concentration of Grief," *AC,* June 4, 1962 and "Those Who Cared for the Important Things," *Life,* June 15, 1962, 39; Semple, "A City Shaken by Tragedy," *The New York Times* [*NY Times*], Jan. 9, 1978; *AC,* May 7, 1962; *AJ,* May 9, 1962; *AJC,* May 6, 1962, Apr. 17, 2001.

Chapter Eight: Martin, *Atlanta and Environs,* 3: 267; Semple, "A City Shaken by Tragedy;" Andrew Sparks, *AJC,* May 6, 1962; Frank Daniel, *AC,* Apr. 30, 1962; Kathryn Grayburn, *AC,* May 10 and June 4, 1962; Jean Rooney, *AC,* Sept. 11, 1962; *AJ,* Apr. 15, 19, 21, 1962.

Chapter Nine: Franklin Garrett, *Yesterday's Atlanta* (Atlanta, GA, 1994), 133; Margaret Turner, *AC*, June 4, 1962; Lockerman, *AC*, June 5, 1962.

Chapter Ten: *AC*, June 4 and 5, 1962.

Chapter Eleven: Allen and Hemphill, *Mayor*, 73-76; *Time:* June 15, 1962; Laura Link, Frank Veale, Frank Wells, C. Sibley and other articles, *AC*, June 4, 1962; Pat Potter, *AJ*, June 5, 1962.

Chapter Twelve: Allen and Hemphill, *Mayor*, 76-80; Patterson, *AC*, June 6 and June 7, 1962; Sam Hopkins, *AJ*, June 4, 1962; Marion Gaines, *AC*, June 5, 1962; Pat Potter *AJ*, June 5, 1962; Achsah Posey, *AC*, June 6, 1962.

Chapter Thirteen: Eugene Patterson, "Atlanta: Tragedy and Resurgence," *Country Beautiful:* Holiday Issue, 1962; Patterson, *AC*, June 5, 1962; Bryans, *AJ*, June 3, 1962; Semple, "A City Shaken by Tragedy;" Lockerman, *AC*, June 12, 1962.

Chapter Fourteen: F. Allen, *Atlanta Rising*, 118-127; Agnew and Duke, "History of the Woodruff Arts Center," 11-25, 36, 78-81; *International Civil Aviation Organization Circular* 71-AN/63, no 12, 1962; Edmunds, *AJC*, Sept. 3, 1981; Posey, *AC*, Mar. 16, June 4, Sept, 17, 1963; Tom Greene and Paul Valentine, *AJ*, Oct. 2, Nov. 18, 26, 1963, May 7, 1964; Patterson, *AC*, Feb. 4, 25, 1965; Ada Louise Huxtable, reprint, *AJC*, Oct. 13, 1968.

Chapter Fifteen: F. Allen, *Atlanta Rising*, 168; Sam Hopkins, *AJC*, June 4, 1972; Barry Henderson, Sam Hopkins, *AC*, Jan. 16, 17, 1978; *NY Times*, Jan. 16, 17, 1968; Burst, *Three Families*, 184-187.

Unpublished Books and Manuscripts

Chapter One: Faye Clarke, "The Atlanta Memorial Arts Center: The Eternal Phoenix" (Ph.D. Dissertation, Georgia State University, 1992), 41-43, 48-50; Robert W. Woodruff Collection, Series 2, Subsection 1, High Museum Collection, Mss. # 664, Scrapbook 2, Boxes 3, 6, 17, 19, 21, 23, Atlanta History Center [Hereafter cited as HMA Collection, AHC].

Chapter Two: Scrapbooks 1 & 2, Mrs. Clifford Ragsdale Papers, AHC.

Chapter Four: Mildred Seydell Papers, Special Collections Robert W. Woodruff Library, Emory University [Hereafter cited as RWW Lib.].

Chapter Five: C. Baxter Jones and Morgan Cantey Papers, Spec. Coll., RWW Lib., Emory; Box 23, HMA Collection, AHC.

Chapter Six: "Every Saturday" file (#615), Atlanta Debutante Scrapbook 1, (#747), AHC.

Chapter Seven: R.W. Woodruff Papers, #10, Box 224, Sp. Coll., RWW Lib., Emory; Box 21, HMA Collection, AHC.

Chapter Nine: Cantey Papers, Seydell Papers, Spec. Coll., RWW Lib., Emory; Scrapbook 2, HMA Collection, AHC.

Chapter Ten: Aubrey Morris Papers, AHC.

Chapter Eleven: Scrapbook 2, HMA Collection, AHC.

Chapter Twelve: Orly and Aubrey Morris Papers, AHC.

Chapter Thirteen: Boxes 3, 23, HMA Collection, AHC.

Chapter Fourteen: Clarke, "The Atlanta Memorial Arts Center," 855-134; R.W. Woodruff Papers, #10, Box 13, Sp. Coll., RWW Lib., Emory; "Catalog of Louvre Exhibition" 1963, HMA Collection, AHC; Skip Goodwin, "On the Occasion of the 25th Anniversary of the Memorial Arts Center."

Chapter Fifteen: Baxter P. Jones, "Arts Deficit: Why it Exists," 2001.

Interviews and Correspondence

Aubrey Morris, former chief of WSB News, and Eugene Patterson, former editor of the *Atlanta Constitution,* were key reporters of the crash in 1962 in both Atlanta and in Paris. Both were kind enough to share their memories with me, as was Doris Lockerman, associate editor of the *Atlanta Constitution.* I owe a special debt of gratitude to Susan Coltrane Lowance and George Goodwin for their helpful insights; and I cannot thank Chris Moser enough for sharing his research, films, photographs, and wisdom.

Relatives of those killed at Orly were most generous in supplying information and agreeing to interviews. A number of the comments came from a meeting with a group of those relatives, October 21, 2000.

I especially want to thank Mary Wyatt Allen, Keith Barnett, Rosa Cogland Baskett, Lee Hill Beck, Milton Bevington, Fred Black, Logan Bleckley III, Harry Boon, Cornelia Whitner Campbell, Morgan Cantey Jr., Nancy Beers Carithers, Steve Clay, Susan Seydel Cofer, Bobbie Cogland, Mary Carver Cox, Nina Crimm, Walt Crimm, William Dilts, Clement Virgin Durkes, Mary C. Fitzhugh, Bob Gerson, Micheline Gerson, Audrey and Jake Goldstein, Jane Stow Greene, Ann Pegram Harris, Penny Armstrong Hart, Inge Hill, Slocum Howland, William Hunnicutt, Baxter P. Jones, Julia Jones, Reese Lanier, Edith Lee, Tom Little Jr., Gregg Loomis, Wesley Martin, Chris McLoughlin Jr., William Merritt Jr., Marti Merritt, Claire Wien Morse, Ann Cantey Paine, Sam Patz, Sarah Anne Patz, Harry Patz, Linda Lanier Ramsey, Charlotte Little Reynolds, Ann Boon Rhea, Emily Jones Rushing, Guerry Barnett Russell, Paul Seydel, Anne Merritt Stembler, Teresa Tidmore Turner, Susan Turner, Frank Virgin, Jane Wellborn, Leonard Wien Jr., Linda Williams, and Carroll Young.

Virginia Adair, Ann Carr, Irene Gerson, Allene Goldsmith, Josephine Robertson, Mary Elizabeth Schroder, Peggy Schiffman, Beverly Taylor, and Nanette West were all generous in sharing memories of their friends and experiences.

Index